Twayne's United States Authors Series

Sylvia E. Bowman, *Editor*

INDIANA UNIVERSITY

Zona Gale

ZONA GALE

by HAROLD P. SIMONSON

University of Puget Sound

Twayne Publishers, Inc. :: New York

MANUFACTURED IN THE UNITED STATES OF AMERICA BY
UNITED PRINTING SERVICES, INC.
NEW HAVEN, CONN.

To
CAROLYN

Preface

IN EVALUATING a writer as little remembered as Zona Gale, the danger of minimizing her work is as great as the curiously tempting one of exaggerating its importance. In the first instance, if a person reads no further than Zona Gale's early Friendship Village stories, he could justifiably relegate her to Nathaniel Hawthorne's "mob of scribbling women." On the other hand, he might assume that because of her nearly three dozen books, essays for some of the nation's leading intellectual magazines, and a Pulitzer Prize in drama, she merits extraordinary acclaim and through the years has been undeservedly neglected.

The present study offers no literary "discovery," nor is its purpose to prove that a prolific writer who won a Pulitzer Prize necessarily deserves special laud. Zona Gale as a minor figure in American literature remains such at the conclusion of this study, the first full-length treatment of her since Mr. August Derleth published his anecdotal biography, *Still Small Voice*, in 1940. To say this, however, is not to belittle her considerable importance. The purpose of this critical study is to review and assess Miss Gale's contribution to American literature. Emphasis is centered upon her writing—its sentimental beginnings to the tart, realistic fiction and drama which briefly put her among the foremost middle western writers of the 1920's, and, still later, to strangely mystical works which reflect her painstaking interest in occultism and spiritual fulfillment. Attention is also given to her literary theories based ambivalently upon both realistic convention and a metaphysical quest.

In tracing Zona Gale's development as a writer, I have thought it necessary to devote considerable attention, especially in Chapter III, to her extra-literary activity. A graduate of the University of Wisconsin, she served as a university regent for many years and received from her alma mater one of her four honorary degrees. As one whose political views were strongly Progressive, she repeatedly campaigned for Wisconsin's Robert M. La Follette, Sr. She was a leader in the Feminist movement and an articulate advocate of pacifism. In short, because her life was intelligently active and much of her writing so firmly rooted in her social and political convictions, this study includes notice of her wide activity beyond Portage, Wisconsin, her birthplace and life-long home town.

In the preparation of this book I am grateful to the State Historical Society of Wisconsin and to the Princeton University Library for making Zona Gale material available to me; special appreciation is due Miss Josephine L. Harper, Manuscripts Librarian, and Mr. Alexander P. Clark, Curator of Manuscripts, at these respective institutions. I am also indebted to Mr. August Derleth who generously allowed my examination of his correspondence with Zona Gale, and to Professor Mark Schorer who replied to several inquiries. Mr. Warren Perry, Miss Elspeth Pope, and Mr. Desmond Taylor, all of the University of Puget Sound Library, assisted me far beyond the call of duty. A Danforth Research Grant made possible trips to both Madison and Portage. Inestimable in value were the anecdotes told years ago by my mother about her own rural Wisconsin childhood.

H. P. S.

University of Puget Sound
Tacoma, Washington

Contents

Chapter

Chronology   11

1.   Portage and Elsewhere   15

2.   Sunshine in Friendship Village   33

3.   Social Action and Politics   51

4.   On to Realism   73

5.   Beyond Realism   93

6.   Theory and Practice   109

7.   Final Years   125

Notes and References   141

Selected Bibliography   147

Index   151

Chronology

1874   Zona Gale born in Portage, Wisconsin, on August 26.

1895   Graduated from the University of Wisconsin.

1895   Joined editorial staff of Milwaukee's *Evening Wisconsin*; eighteen months later joined staff of Milwaukee *Journal*.

1901   Became a reporter for the New York *Evening World*.

1902   Employed as Edmund Clarence Stedman's secretary; associated with writers in the Stedman literary circle, including Richard Le Gallienne and Ridgely Torrence.

1904   Returned to Portage and broke off romance with Torrence after nearly two years of courtship.

1906   Published first novel, *Romance Island*.

1910   Won $2000 as first prize in *The Delineator* short fiction contest.

1912- Participated in numerous activities: Wisconsin Dramatic
1920   Society, civic projects, pacifism, women's suffrage, La Follette progressivism in Wisconsin, reform legislation.

1921   Won Pulitzer Prize for *Miss Lulu Bett* (the play).

1922   Received her first honorary degree: Doctor of Letters from Ripon College.

1923   May 29, mother died; appointed by Governor John Blaine to University of Wisconsin's Board of Regents.

1924   Campaigned for La Follette, Sr., on the third-party ticket.

1925   Influenced the selection of Glenn Frank as president of University of Wisconsin.

1927   Joined "Save Sacco and Vanzetti!" movement.

1927- Traveled to California and visited Frank Miller's Mission
1928   Inn.

1928   Married William L. Breese of Portage; adopted three-year-old Leslyn.

1929 September 18, father died; received honorary degree from University of Wisconsin.

1930 Received honorary degree from Rollins College, Winter Park, Florida; covered Republican National Convention in Chicago for Milwaukee *Journal.*

1933 Appointed as Wisconsin's representative to the International Congress of Women in Chicago.

1936 Embroiled in controversy over Glenn Frank's dismissal at University of Wisconsin.

1937 Traveled to Japan.

1938 December 27, died in Chicago hospital; December 30, buried in Silver Lake cemetery, Portage.

1939 Posthumous publication of *Magna.*

Zona Gale

CHAPTER *1*

Portage and Elsewhere

I

THE TWO WORDS "Portage, Wisconsin" signified life to Zona Gale. There she was born and there she was secured by ties of home and parents. These two words, written by her thousands of times, became "charged," she said, in a way unknown to the casual visitor. "It seems strange," she wrote in 1928, ten years before her death, "that the majority of the people in the United States have never heard of [Portage]."[1] Though frequently away from it, she always returned. After coming back from a winter in New York, her second favorite city, she wrote to Hamlin Garland: "It is quite heavenly here, after my joyous season of brick and mortar."[2] Garland, on the other hand, thought it "a drab little city,"[3] but he correctly observed that Zona Gale's imagination transformed its drabness into literature. The extent of her success may be told in Willa Cather's reaction to the town of Zona Gale's fiction: "I am haunted by Portage."[4]

Zona Gale, like many American writers, found in small-town life the distillation of American folkways. Since Colonial times, native writers with a strong sense for locality have sought to identify the nation itself by delineating specific regions representative of American manners. Small communities, originally left in the wake of frontier expansion, held abundant material for local colorists who in the North, South, and West celebrated their own provinciality.

The Middle West had its own regionalists, who, by the 1870's, had begun to set the dominant tone which later writers followed. The best word to describe this tone is "sullen," for the representative works point again and again, both subtly and ponderously, to this quality. Joseph Kirkland, Edward Eggleston, E. W. Howe, Edgar Lee Masters, Sherwood Anderson, Sinclair

Lewis—each in his own way, and Zona Gale in hers—showed the post-frontier communities as being far this side of paradise. The monotony, social and emotional curbing, tastelessness, cultural poverty, pettiness, and general stagnation took the place of what had been for the first discoverers a mythical garden. The local colorists, who came next, found more often an atmosphere of disillusionment; as a region the Middle West became for writers "a metaphor of abuse."[5]

But life is not one tone, not even on Main Street. Zona Gale was justified in pointing out this fact, though some of her efforts at sweetness and light turned into innocuous puffballs fully deserving the criticism they received. The point, however, is that her acid little novels like *Miss Lulu Bett* and *Faint Perfume* present only part of her view. Not all her characters are singular American boobs, not all are Philistines. Even Sinclair Lewis showed his Sam Dodsworth to be a man of backbone, and many of Sherwood Anderson's "grotesques" hide an uncanny beauty. In sympathy with such writers as Ruth Suckow, Ole Rölvaag, and Willa Cather, Zona Gale wrote stories about people knit firmly together by common ties of sacrifice, humor, perseverance, and tragedy. To read her prolific work is to discover a surprisingly polychromatic writer whose little town of Portage, called by Carl Van Doren "one of the sweetest of all literary villages,"[6] is large enough to embrace a multitude of townsmen and manners.

Portage, then, takes its place with Lewis' Zenith and Gopher Prairie, Anderson's Winesburg, and Carl Van Vechten's Maple Valley. In each town the main street sliced through a cross-section of provincial America. The drama to be seen brought the small town into American literature to stay. It is true that neither Zona Gale's fame nor sensationalism equalled that of many other realists. But it is well to remember that her widely read novel *Miss Lulu Bett*, exactly contemporaneous with Lewis' *Main Street*, was hardly less influential in establishing the new direction in provincial realism; and it won for her a Pulitzer Prize when she adapted it for the stage in 1921.

II

It is difficult to imagine a daughter more attached to parents than Zona Gale was to Charles and Eliza Gale. Absence, romantic love, career—nothing but death could sever these three: the death of her mother, in 1923, when Zona Gale was forty-nine and of her father, in 1929, when she was fifty-five. As a spinster until the age of fifty-four, when she soberly married William L. Breese, a Portage stocking manufacturer, she quietly worshiped her parents and saw herself in their constant judgment. When Eliza died, she was deprived of her anchor, and for many years she wandered in mystical ways filling notebooks with "spirit messages" from her. Her father's death, preceding her own by nine years, left her alone. Neither her husband, her step-daughter Juliette, nor her adopted daughter Leslyn alleviated her losses.

She had early discovered her father's reflective and meditative character. Though he was not college-trained, he possessed a sturdy library of Shakespeare, Spenser, Darwin, Emerson, Drummond, and Bacon. He enjoyed reading philosophy and often stated to her that Plato's *Phaedo* and the writings of Emanuel Swedenborg best defined his own belief in philosophic idealism. "That there are between man and that which is outside him, certain correspondences" indicates the kind of aphorisms he continually jotted on stray envelopes, time-cards, and lunch-counters. He pencilled into small, pocket-sized notebooks such inscriptions as:

All laws are friendly to those who obey them.

* * *

Children early catch the tone of their surroundings.

* * *

Most people are unhappy because they have no information concerning the real sources of enjoyment.

* * *

Until men grow up to the level of a higher life they cannot receive it.

* * *

Everything exists for something else of a higher order.[7]

To Zona Gale these scribblings and numberless little essays about the Higher Life showed that a person like her father (who was a railroad engineer for forty-three years) was not handicapped by educational limitations. The transcendental spirit was not monopolized in academic circles, she insisted, repeatedly writing what became for her a creed: "Life is something more than that which we believe it to be." Something of this spiritual freedom suggested itself to her when she remembered that, as a child, she and her father one frosty morning saw some sparrows eating grain spilled from a boxcar. When the two approached, all the birds flew away but one, whose foot was stuck fast to the cold steel track. Her father, she remembered, held his hand on the little foot until it was warm; then, like a freed spirit, the bird also flew away.

She herself was physically fragile; many friends commented on her incredibly small wrists and hands. Her father was also slight and small-boned. Of Scotch-Irish descent, he represented the eighth generation of Gales in America. Richard Gale (the name was orginally spelled Gael, even after the family came to America) settled in Watertown, Massachusetts, in 1640. Henry Gale, of the fifth generation, fought in the Revolutionary Army's victory over Burgoyne in 1777. In 1787 he led his company as a captain in Shays' Rebellion against the state of Massachusetts and its federal arsenal at Springfield. For this "indiscretion" he was convicted of treason and sentenced to be shot. After a reprieve, then a pardon, he homesteaded in Vermont.

Zona Gale's father, Charles, was born on August 25, 1842, in Galetown, Ohio, near Clyde, the birthplace of Sherwood Anderson. When he was six, his father died; when seven, his mother. At the age of nineteen he struck off for the northern woods, and arrived in Portage in March, 1861. He had intended to stay only two weeks, but his new job with the Chicago, Milwaukee and St. Paul railroad and, particularly, his assignment to drive an engine of his own, held him longer. Restlessness and youth led him to still other jobs in Missouri and Pennsylvania, but he returned to Portage in 1867, resumed his job with the railroad, and then in 1872, when thirty-two, married Eliza Beers. Two years later, on August 26, Zona was born, their first and only child.

Her mother, Eliza Beers Gale, exerted a strange influence over Zona. As the years passed, the daughter remained within the orbit of her mother's watchfulness. The relationship was extraordinarily tight, so much so that Zona's other relationships, especially that in her late twenties with the poet Ridgely Torrence, never flourished because of Eliza's subtle dominance. As Zona Gale matured, she vaguely perceived that something akin to a Mother Principle was the core of life: a fecundity serving to unify nature into a single symbol. So attracted was she to this symbol, represented to her by Eliza, that to alienate herself from it was to suffer guilt. She wrote at the time of her mother's death that now her name, Eliza Beers Gale, becomes "a still deeper symbol of mystery in which we share."[8] With Eliza's death (she was seventy-seven) Zona Gale's pain radically re-directed her literary efforts into the mysticism of *Preface to a Life,* written three years later. To an unpublished collection of poetry entitled *Flight of Clouds* she added such "Mother" poems as "I Heard Her Weeping in the Night," "I Wish I Had Said More," and "When First, With Cry of Some Remembered Pain." One of them, "My Mother Is What Beauty Was to Me," most characteristically indicates their theme:

> My mother is what beauty was to me
> When I was young. Then I would step serene
> Where wanly shadow lay along the green
> Like ashes of the light, and almost see
> Strange incense from strange altars ceaselessly
> Go up to God like souls. And I would lean,
> An acolyte of dreams, till the unseen
> Had all but set my brooding spirit free.
>
> Thus richly were my days distilled to years
> Dissolving pearls of pain. One dusk I went
> Seeking far loveliness in some near guise
> And finding but old faces with new tears.
> But oh, one walked and watched with me! I bent
> And read all beauty in her quiet eyes.

Born in the town of Cuba, New York, on October 31, 1846, Eliza Beers was one of five children. Her father, Thomas Cook Beers, had grown up in Pittsford, New York, and her mother, Harriet (Taylor) Beers, had emigrated from Sussex County, England, in 1832. When Eliza was twelve, her father died, and Harriet, with her three daughters and two sons, moved to Middleton Junction, Wisconsin, where her father, Joseph Taylor, had a farm. The small band of mother and five children arrived only to see the fresh grave of Joseph who had died while they were en route. His wife, Constance Hoath Taylor, had been buried several years before. Harriet and the children stayed on the farm with the two sons of Joseph and Constance, and it was here that Eliza spent her childhood.

Anxious to leave the farm which she hated, Eliza earned a teaching certificate from the district school and, when only fifteen, taught at neighboring Pine Bluff. With her savings of a hundred dollars for the year, she entered Tullis Academy in Madison. After the outbreak of the Civil War and the departure of her brothers, she returned to Middleton Junction to help support her mother and two sisters, one of whom was early widowed and left with a son to support because of the war. Maintaining the farm was now impossible, so again they moved, this time to Portage where the three sisters opened a dressmaking shop. Eliza, finished with her studies at the Portage high school, met Charles Gale in 1867, and the five-year courtship ended in marriage a month before she was twenty-eight.

With no brothers or sisters, Zona Gale turned to her parents and to herself. As a child she showed little interest in robust sports. Her favorite game, called The Deep Woods, she played merely by retiring to a corner of a room and hiding behind an open umbrella. She said to Sumner Keene in 1921 that her first recollection of anything that happened as a child was "of stepping over a threshold and entering another room."9 Safe within, behind her umbrella, she lived in a world of enchantment which no one disturbed. It was not until she was eight that she walked the short way to town alone (to buy a spool of white thread, number fifty) and saw, for the first time, her solitary shadow on the wooden paving blocks of the street.

As she repeatedly said, Portage itself had an "enchanting" name, comparable to "hermitage." To her, something make-believe vitalized this town edging the Wisconsin River. The Indian name Wisconsin (Ouisconsin) meant "black rushing water," signifying that the river was dark and powerful, though it flows serenely by Portage. As a girl she listened to stories about the arrival of Jean Joliet and Father Marquette who first crossed from the Fox to the Wisconsin River in 1673 and established the portage. The lore too included the Winnebagos who built giant bonfires in the main street and danced around them all night; and Red Bird, the young Winnebago chief, who killed a white family whom he thought responsible for a wrong to his tribe and who, when discovering his mistake, returned to Portage and gave himself up; and Yellow Thunder who was murdered on Cook Street; and Pauquette, the first white child in the town, who was so strong in his youth that when one of his oxen broke loose in the center of the Wisconsin River, he yoked himself into his load and swam ashore.[10]

Portage also held the history of Old Fort Winnebago, built on the site of a John Jacob Astor fur trading post. Both President Zachary Taylor and Jefferson Davis were stationed there at different times in the 1850's. Portage had other connections too: with Mrs. Abraham Lincoln and "Tad," who spent a summer at nearby Devil's Lake; with John Muir, whose birthplace and farm house were only a short distance east of town; with Frederick Jackson Turner, who left Portage to become one of America's great nineteenth-century historians. Portage also meant childhood taffy-pulls, buggy-rides about town, Christmas programs in the church basement, and Fourth of July music and speeches in the small, triangular park adjacent to the school. As a child Zona Gale absorbed Portage; later she sought to understand it.

Her early years are best recorded in her girlhood accounts kept in notebooks, tablets, or—in the case of her first "book" written at the age of seven—on brown wrapping paper. One story, written when she was eight, starts: "It was a cold bleak October day. The snow fell thickly, covering the city of Elmhurst. Until it looked like a great snowbank. The wind blew in cold, fitful, gusts from the north-east. The streets were deserted. No, not entirely, for a slight figure was stealing its way down the avenue." In the same notebook is a poem called Spring:

> Spring! the fairest of all seasons,
>   Come again, come again.
> For wanting you we've many reasons,
>   Come again, come again.
>
> Sweet violet & May flower,
>   Come again, come again.
> Come deck each sunny bower
>   Come again, come again.
>
> And oh! dear little butter-cup,
>   Come again, come again.
> To me turning your sweet face up,
>   Come again, come again.

But O! there is no use calling
    You are gone, you are gone.
Now the Autumn leaves are falling;
    You are gone, you are gone.

At twelve she was tempted to submit for publication a story about a beautiful duchess. The next year she finished a "novel" called "A White Dove," which her mother re-copied for her and sent to *Youth's Companion*. She remembered that it came back the same week. In other notebooks she wrote plot summaries of books she had read. One notebook, which bears the label, "From Eleven Years Old and Upwards," includes summaries of John Bunyan's *The Pilgrim's Progress*, Charles Dickens' *Dombey and Son* and *Nicholas Nickleby*, Charles Kingsley's *Hypatia*, R. D. Blackmore's *Lorna Doone*, and George Eliot's *The Mill on the Floss*. Other lists and notes mention works of E. P. Roe, Louisa May Alcott, Sir Walter Scott, Francis Burnett, William Thackeray, Lew Wallace, Rider Haggard, Lord Bulwer-Lytton, and Nathaniel Hawthorne.

Her childhood in Portage was briefly interrupted when the family moved first to Delano, Minnesota; later to St. Paul (in both places her father's plans for business failed); and then back to Portage, to the railroad, and to their house on Conant Street—where Zona Gale's childhood memories were fixed. Mr. August Derleth, in his biography of her, places considerable importance upon the fact that during these young years she "never danced," "seldom played outside games," and was a "lonely figure" who cared little for boys.[11] Her childhood, however, was not unhappy. While naturally retiring, she enjoyed to the fullest her friendship with Edith Rogers and the games and studies they shared.

In 1891 she enrolled in the University of Wisconsin. In 1923 Governor John Blaine appointed her as a university regent; in 1929, she was awarded an honorary degree by the University and, in 1935, was elected by the regents to the Board of Visitors. But no hint of her future influence was evident during her undergraduate years. In fact, in her sophomore year she tried to leave, and she would have left had her parents been less firm in keeping her where she was. Unlike her childhood years in Portage where she was not bothered by her lack of "popularity," she confronted for the first time the arbitrarily created loyalties of the University's sorority system, with its artificial inequalities which "made" one's popularity. Such was her distaste for sororities that, many years later, she wrote to the student editor of the University's *Cardinal* (June 3, 1918):

> I hope that no one will mind too much my questionable taste in admitting that the sorority situation clouded my own university life to such a degree that, much as I love the campus, I never go back there without experiencing again, through memory, something of the unhappiness of those days which ought to have been happy. . . . It used to be the fashion for those of us who were without the benefits of the sororities to keep up a pretence that all this did not matter. But we all knew that it did matter. And it seems to me that it must matter now, and that it will always matter, must as all inequalities matter.

More scars would later mark her carefully nurtured innocence, and their number led to an acute social consciousness. When in April, 1926, she again wrote on sororities, she asserted that "self-magnification is ridiculous" and that "the admission of a self-superiority, even when it is true, becomes at last the great illusion. Why? Because nobody can continue to assert that he is better than others and continue to remain so. There is some secret and scrupulous law which attends to this."[12]

Madison was her first step away from idyllic Portage. To be sure, it was not a big step. When, for example, she received a three-dollar check for her first published story entitled "Both," printed in a Milwaukee newspaper, she was so thrilled that she took the noon train back home (forty miles) to exhibit the check to her proud parents and then returned to school two hours later. Yet her world was expanding. At the University she made a good record, especially in English. She wrote steadily through her four years and submitted work to the University's literary magazine, *The Aegis*, as well as to magazines and newspapers. Nothing was accepted in the magazines, but the Portage *Democrat* printed some of her writing and she won two literary prizes at the University for an essay and a poem.

After graduating in 1895 she took another step, this one to Milwaukee where she was determined to become a self-supporting journalist. By appearing every morning for two weeks to ask the editor of the *Evening Wisconsin* if there was anything to be written that day, she was finally given occasional assignments. Later she joined the staff at fifteen dollars a week, an even more thrilling success, she remembered, than the three-dollar check. She interviewed celebrities, covered weddings and plays, made the usual rounds among the ladies' clubs, and on one occasion met Jane Addams whose work at Hull House in Chicago excited her. The hurly-burly newspaper office in Milwaukee sharply contrasted with this new feminine reporter who seemed too slender, too frail.

The modest girl from Portage soon enjoyed the reputation for untiring energy. Eighteen months later an even better position opened with the Milwaukee *Journal* where she was given more important assignments. Among her associates on the staff she was thought to be a model reporter. Even after she left the newspaper in 1901 to join the staff of the New York *Evening World* her name was not forgotten in Milwaukee. When Edna Ferber started on the *Journal* after Zona Gale had left, she heard the name so often repeated that she grew "to hate the sound of it."[13] Then one day she met Miss Gale and was struck by her "great dark tragic eyes in a little pointed face; the gentlest of voices; a hand so tiny that when one took it in one's grasp it felt like the crushing of a bird's wing."[14] She appeared to Edna Ferber as one unequipped to contend in a society rapidly taking shape according to the principles of social Darwinism. She seemed as dangerously out of place as Mary French in Dos Passos' *The Big Money.*

When Zona Gale left Wisconsin in 1901 she was following the tradition of other Middle West writers who went east either to escape small-town monotony or to seek their real education. One thinks of William Dean Howells, Willa Cather, Sherwood Anderson, Floyd Dell, Hamlin Garland, and even folksy Ruth Suckow. Some did not return, as was the case of Glenway Wescott, whose pen was dipped in acid when he wrote *Good-Bye Wisconsin* (1928). Zona Gale returned—to the very house she left. But before retracing her steps, she journeyed even farther away.

Breaking into the newspaper game in New York required the same persistence she had shown in Milwaukee. The invariable reply from the editors would be "no vacancy on the staff," though each editor kindly scribbled her name and address on a scrap for his files. Knowing she would receive no assignments just by waiting to be called, she repeated her visits and offered lists of news items, special features, and interviews which she suggested the editors assign her to write. She did this every day whether any were checked or not. At the end of several weeks the New York *Evening World* began giving her space assignments. Soon thereafter she became a full-time reporter, "as beautiful as any girl could be,"[15] covering a downtown beat that included murders and practically everything else. Her picture often accompanied her stories, "too repeatedly," some said enviously.[16]

The grape had burst, and she grew heady with success. For a year and a half the little charmer from Portage reveled in the whirl of the New York newspaper office, and among a host of new friends were Isadora Duncan, Walter Damrosch, John Burroughs, and Louis Untermeyer. Among them was the Englishman Richard Le Gallienne who, after only three years in New York, was regarded as another bohemian Oscar Wilde. Zona Gale wrote to her parents about him, little suspecting that each letter stung them and increased their wish for her to return to Portage. With misgivings about her daughter's life in faraway New York, Eliza Gale inquired, "Have I taught you right?" and then added, "Of course now you are a *lady*, and if I have failed in my teaching it is because I was lacking in knowing the right."

Later Eliza pleaded with her to return: "Come on home Zona, where you can be warm if you stay in the house." She frequently hinted to Zona about the consequences of entanglements: "I had a long conversation with your little slippers that are still in my bedroom by the stand where you left them. I love them because your dear little feet have been in them. Those dear little feet that I tried so hard to make walk in the path that leads to all goodness, purity, and love—*good* love." The innuendoes were obvious enough. By 1903 Eliza's hints became direst warnings: "Womanhood is a trophy, and indeed it is, when temptations are all around us—nothing but the power of God can keep any of us, and when we grow away from Him we have not the strength we would have if we only live close *close* to Him." Dutifully uneasy, Zona Gale wrote little messages in return, often no more than "did um cry when um read about the party?" or "Now lovie and lovie and lovie. Good night. Babe."[17]

Her parents grew even more agitated when Zona Gale quit the *Evening World* to free-lance. While on the paper's reportorial staff she had spent long evenings writing fiction but had sold none of it. Then almost simultaneously *Outing, Smart Set,* and *Success* magazines accepted stories. Charles Hanson Towne, who at that time was editor of *Smart Set,* remembered in his memoirs that Zona Gale's distinguishing marks were, again, persistence and energy.[18] Her literary career had now begun.

Actually its outset was marked less by published work than by new literary friends. Richard Le Gallienne had introduced her to Edmund Clarence Stedman who, in turn, invited her to attend his regular Sunday Club at his home "Casa Laura" in Bronxville. To these Sunday afternoon and evening gatherings came many young writers: William Vaughn Moody, Ridgely Torrence, Edwin Arlington Robinson, Beatrice Demarest Lloyd and David Lloyd, Charles Hanson Towne, Harriet Monroe, Yone Naguchi. While the Stedmans themselves epitomized literary conservatism, the others were youthful bibliophiles and experimenters who encouraged Zona Gale at every turn.

Serving as Stedman's personal secretary during the summer of 1902 had made it possible for her to leave the newspaper in order to free-lance; but more importantly, this was the summer she fell in with Ridgely Torrence, fourteen months younger than herself at twenty-eight.

III

A study of Zona Gale and her work should include mention of her deep ardor for Torrence. Only a few of her contemporaries knew anything about it; critics of her work have seldom referred to him, and Mr. Derleth skims over the whole subject. There is, however, in the Princeton University Library a collection bequeathed by Torrence of over one hundred and fifty letters written to him by Zona Gale. Evidence from these letters brings to light both an astonishing relationship and a pivotal experience in Zona Gale's life. The fact that she, like Emily Dickinson, remained silent about her failure in love, except as she attempted to universalize it through art, suggests the intensity of the original experience. Like the Amherst poet, she also tried to forget by "sweeping up the heart/And putting love away/We shall not want to use again/Until eternity." Throughout her years

of literary work she said nothing about Torrence, as she joined
many of her contemporaries (Sarah Orne Jewett, Amy Lowell,
Ellen Glasgow, Sara Teasdale, Willa Cather) in spinsterhood.

Her only love had been for Ridgely Torrence who, like herself,
had come from a small Midwestern town to try his fortune in
New York. Born and reared in Xenia, in southwestern Ohio,
Torrence had left behind the mercantile interests of his parents
when he enrolled at age eighteen in Miami University in Oxford,
Ohio. Brilliant but exceptionally temperamental, he could not
wait until he was graduated to go east. He transferred to
Princeton as a junior, in the class of 1897, but he left without
a degree to take a job in the Astor Library in New York. In
1901 he accepted an appointment as librarian in the Lenox
Library where he stayed until 1903. For the next two years he
did editorial work for the *Critic,* then took another editorial
job for two more years with the *Cosmopolitan.* All the while he
was hobnobbing in the Stedman group and writing verse resembling Edward Fitzgerald's version of Omar Khayyam. After
Torrence's one hundred quatrains were published as *The House
of a Hundred Lights* (1900), Stedman paternally honored him
with a place in his *An American Anthology: 1787-1900* (1900),
a collection which later proved one of the most instrumental in
establishing the fact of a national poetry.

It was at "Casa Laura" (named after Mrs. Laura Stedman) in
Bronxville that Torrence and Zona Gale met in 1902. Both of them
had tasted the sweetness of initial literary success and both
were ambitious for more. Neither was aware that ten years
earlier Herman Melville, a literary orphan, had died in this
same city which was now beguiling them. Nor is there reason
to suppose they knew the characters of Maggie, the Bowery
destitutes, or George's mother in the pages of Stephen Crane
who, at twenty-nine, had died the year before Zona Gale came
to his city. Instead of these writers, or Zola, or the later Howells,
Torrence and Zona Gale chose to admire the fantasies of Maurice
Maeterlinck and the limpid, lifeless art of Swinburne, Rossetti,
Khayyam, and Theophile Gautier, whose famous dictum of "art
for art's sake" set the tone.

At first, letters from Bronxville to the Lenox Library showed
the restraint of "Dear Mr. Torrence," but soon the heading became much more affectionate. Like the belated Romantics who,

with Oscar Wilde and his flamboyant admirers, sought to sublimate the world in art, Zona Gale rhapsodized her feelings like
a typical *fin de siècle* aesthete. Thoughts of Torrence were to
her like something rarified and ethereal; his spirit, she said,
accompanied her wherever she went. During that ecstatic summer
and autumn, letters between the two of them contained the
shimmering language of lovers. From time to time the unpleasant
note from Portage sounded to remind her of sin and practicality.
"Seems to me, you and Mr. Torrence are pretty good friends,"
her mother wrote. "What is he doing or is he a *dreamer* that will
do for some but won't buy the dress or food. You said he left the
place he was and it is we *dined* and we *dined*. Who pays the
price?" Unruffled in breaking away from Portage society, Zona
Gale blithely continued with Torrence; in November, 1902, she
wrote she was even acquiring a taste for sherry.

In an idealistic romance, lovers should be separated for their
affections to grow stronger. In November an old acquaintance
from Madison, a Mrs. Adams, who was dying in Redlands,
California, offered to pay Miss Gale's expenses to nurse her
during her last days. Separated from Torrence by four thousand
miles, she wrote long letters about the nature of ideal love.
Much like a Botticelli nun—anathema to a D. H. Lawrence—
Zona Gale disembodied her emotions by confessing that Torrence's spirit, not his manliness, drew her to him. Amid her
gilt-edged, flowery volumes of Maeterlinck and Rossetti, she
thought herself a Blessed Damozel sending kisses of California
lemon-blossoms to her lover.

After Mrs. Adams died, Zona Gale promised Torrence to
return to him after a brief stopover in San Francisco. A month
later she was still in San Francisco, her circle of literary acquaint-
ances including Will Irwin of the *Chronicle*, Frank Gelett Burgess, Ward McAllister, and Gertrude Atherton's family. She explained to Torrence that she was wildly enchanted with San
Francisco; in another letter she assured him that her delay in
returning only intensified her feelings for him. In her exuberance
she even teased her long-suffering knight with the thought that
she might not return at all; soon thereafter she gave her word
that she would dine with him in New York within a month.

On her way to New York she stopped at Portage. She was
home for the first time in two years. Writing to Torrence about

this fact, she wondered if he realized the importance of her being home—alone with her mother and father. She cautiously avoided talking to them about her affection for Torrence, suspecting what their feelings were and being herself somewhat unsure about her own. When she returned to New York in February, he was eagerly waiting for her, and during the next several months they saw each other almost daily. Almost as frequently, Zona received letters from Eliza Gale, who persisted in her efforts to weld the family triangle even more tightly. "I thank Him," she wrote to her daughter, "for the lovely soul he gave to the dearest daughter He ever gave anyone called by the world Zona Gale but by me an angel of love, *love* greater than any one knows only just Papa and me and you too." By August, when Zona Gale left for a vacation at Lake Placid, she was ready to quit playing the love-game with Torrence and to marry him. On August 20, from Montreal, she at last consented in writing to marry him; she wished, in fact, to do so immediately.

Torrence, who had just finished his poetic drama *El Dorado*, was awaiting its production in the fall. Therefore, he suggested that the marriage be postponed for a few months, for, with the new theater season, he would have some money. In the meantime he supposed himself engaged to her and proceeded to tell some of his friends, including Stedman. Upon learning what he had done, Miss Gale, inexplicably chilled, wrote him that she did not want anything done until she had another talk with Portage.

Determined to resolve the subject once and for all, she immediately returned home. Yet her confusion and doubts kept her from even mentioning Torrence's name during the first week after her arrival. Tormented by both skin rash and insomnia, she wrote on September 16 that she had finally not only mentioned him but also the possibility of his visiting Portage, But, she added, "I don't know how I am ever in this *world* going to say that I love you. I can't bear anything that gives them pain. I suppose I'm weak about it, but I can't bear it. My throat is all bothered up just writing about it. O dear—and I wanted it so. . . . Well dear, I guess I'm married already—to Portage."[19]

The whole affair still unresolved because she could not explain her feelings to her parents, she returned to New York even further tortured by her dilemma between Torrence and Portage. Throughout the spring she and Torrence continued weighing,

testing, trying to believe that something could be settled. He
had begun writing his next drama, published in 1907 as *Abelard
and Heloise*, while she continued writing short fiction for the
magazines. She returned to Portage in August to celebrate her
thirtieth birthday and, fatefully, to learn the outcome of her
dilemma. Earlier she had wanted Torrence to visit her at
Portage. When his telegram arrived stating that he would
definitely come later in the month (Eliza had insisted that he
should not come until after Zona's birthday so that the three of
them might celebrate the occasion alone), she knew the climax
was at hand. The afternoon of the telegram she had been playing
flinch with her mother, but when the telegram was delivered she
remembered that a most curious silence fell, as if her dear
mother had lost all spirit.

One needs only to read these daily letters to Torrence to
realize how close Zona Gale came to nervous breakdown. She
lashed him for saying he wanted first to seek advice from mutual
friends before coming. Then, after self-abasement for this vio-
lence against him, she impetuously fled from home to spend three
days regaining her equilibrium in Galloway, a tiny village in the
northern Wisconsin woods eighty miles from Portage. What was
akin to a near-mystical experience, she eloquently described in
subsequent letters as her awakening to a new sense of morality,
beauty, and spirit. Comparing her experience to that of Henry
James's Lambert Strether in *The Ambassadors,* she described her
illumination, her redemption by love, in the most impassioned
prose she ever was to write, flaming and yet beautifully con-
densed.

Exhilarated beyond words, she returned from the woods forti-
fied to leave home and parents and to go with Torrence should
he wish to marry her now. Ironically, she never had the chance
to act upon this decision which had cost her so much. When
Torrence arrived in Portage, he informed her that he had discovered, to his complete surprise, that during the preceding
spring in New York she regularly had been seeing Richard
Le Gallienne, the English poet and habitué of the Stedman
group. Zona confessed the truth: that she and Le Gallienne had
met often that spring; that from the start, back in 1901, she was
simply lonely for companionship and Le Gallienne's charm and
intelligence had intrigued her; that she had never loved him; and,

finally, that to have told the truth earlier would have been to invite Torrence to infer what was not true. Torrence, however, could not understand why she had continued seeing Le Gallienne if she had not been fond of him. With double irony, even Mama Gale now sought to convince Torrence that her "little girl" had loved him all along but, unfortunately, had met "wicked men" in New York. She blamed her daughter's "would be friends" for having allowed her to "drift and drift." Referring to her daughter's arch tempter, Le Gallienne, she wrote to Torrence, "There is a *Hell* for men like him."

Zona Gale did not resolve the tension by merely returning to her Portage home. Anxieties are rarely lessened so easily when they earlier had absorbed so much of one's emotional life. Ten years later, in 1914, Torrence married Olivia Howard Dunbar. Twenty years later, still occasionally corresponding with him, Miss Gale confessed that to her he remained incomparable. "I do hope," she wrote, "that in our next incarnation we can be lovers again— and, *that* time, have enough more star-dust, in me, to bring it off." After the cataclysmic autumn of 1904 she bent her total effort in literary, social, political, and educational work. Among her achievements during the ensuing thirty-four years were thirty separate books of fiction, poetry, and drama besides scores of other publications. One wonders how different her output would have been if her thirtieth birthday had been followed by marriage to Ridgely Torrence.

CHAPTER 2

Sunshine in Friendship Village

I

IMMEDIATELY AFTER Zona Gale's romance with Ridgely Torrence had changed from melodrama to painful involvement and then to failure, she went to New York, not to continue seeing Richard Le Gallienne, but to remain in the romantic afterglow of the Stedman circle where the exotic old-century aura of stale smoke and wilted chrysanthemums still lingered. She hardly knew why such aesthetes as Edgar Saltus and James Huneker preferred the old to the new. She was not seriously knowledgeable about the mauve world of Stéphane Mallarmé and Baudelaire, nor did she understand why Edmond Rostand had escaped into the historic past and Pierre Loti into remote and exotic lands. She had read the English Pre-Raphaelites and the aesthetes of the 1890's, led by Oscar Wilde and Aubrey Beardsley, but she did not share the militancy of these writers in preserving the autonomy of both art and the artist against mercantilism and literary realism. Tolstoy and the Haymarket Riot, which shocked William Dean Howells into social consciousness, were as yet outside her ken; so too were Zola, Flaubert, and Dreiser's *Sister Carrie*.

From her letters and early short stories one finds little to show her awareness that both Europe and America were moving through crises. There had been England's humiliation in its questionable victory over the Boers, followed by the German claims in Morocco in 1905, Austria's annexation of Bosnia in 1908, and the whole ineffectual effort to quell the growing agitation of Germany and her partners. On this side of the Atlantic, America's imperialism was less than manifestly moral. The colored slaves in the South had been emancipated earlier, but they were being tracked down by Fire Eaters; in the North the wage-slaves were in worse bondage than ever. For a pet, one American capitalist maintained a midget on a leash; another preached that people, like rosebuds, must be pruned in order that a few may flourish. The 400 Club danced to "Ta-ra-ra-boom-de-ay" and lighted cigars with one hundred dollar bills; the average worker's wage in the 1890's was two dollars a day. And so, while the new century was being heralded by Frank Norris' *The Pit* (1903), Upton Sinclair's *The Jungle* (1906), and Jane Addams' *Twenty Years at Hull House* (1910), and while that most sombre of all books—*The Education of Henry Adams*—privately signaled in 1907 the fatal outcome of the brave, new century, Zona Gale in New York busily started her first novel, *Romance Island* (1906).

Stedman, who called the book "diaphanous" and "exquisite," was convinced that his protégée had proved herself a skilled writer. He confessed having enjoyed wonder-tales since he was five years old; *Romance Island,* he said, beguiled him from the "weary work-a-day life."[1] Zona Gale had patently succeeded in her purpose, for, true to the dictum of Wilde ("The first duty of life is to be as artificial as possible"),[2] she had avoided the close-at-hand in order to be as unnatural (and romantic) as possible.

The name that Romance Island would bear on a navigator's map—if it were four-dimensional—would be Yaque. It would be intuited somewhere south of the Azores and necessarily inaccessible to people having the navigational limitations of mere reason. Its Prince Tabnit has arrived in New York to tell Miss Olivia Holland that her father, previously taken to Yaque and crowned King Otho I, has recently disappeared with the hereditary fortune of the island. Olivia goes with Prince Tabnit to Yaque, and what follows is an incredibly tangled plot in which the Prince finally emerges the villain.

Secretly following Prince Tabnit and Olivia is St. George who arrives at Yaque in time to hear Prince Tabnit announce his engagement to Olivia. St. George wisely suspects the Prince's evil design in luring Olivia to the island. He learns that the Prince himself has hidden the Yaque gold and that, by means of a magic potent, he has transformed Mr. Holland into an unidentifiable old man. But on the day Prince Tabnit is to marry Olivia, Mr. Holland, alias King Otho I, reappears, freed from the potent's effect. Tabnit's treachery revealed, the Prince drinks the same miraculous wine and escapes as an old man into the crowd. Mr. Holland rejoins Olivia and, happily, all return to New York on St. George's yacht, the same that will soon take St. George and Olivia on their honeymoon.

Zona Gale frequently told young writers about the difficulty she had in selling her early short stories. Although she would add demurely that her first novel, *Romance Island*, was accepted right off, she had justifiable qualms about its merit. Occasional moments of suspense fail to relieve the cloying sentimentality. Her growing interest in occultism and telepathy is awkwardly handled in the novel. Mechanical characterizations match her flat style which even annoyed Stedman who pointed out such impossible expressions as "enough to fleet the time," "to homage them," and "never marvelled its way."[3] Despite manifest faults, the book drew from reviewers the typical laudatory cant which often deceives young writers into thinking that their work is not so badly written as it actually may be. "I don't remember another book by an American woman, with the rare imagination, the grace and brave originality of this one," a reviewer wrote in the San Francisco *Bulletin* (Dec. 2, 1906). Fresh from this kind of encouragement, meaningless as it was, Miss Gale immediately started her next book, *The Loves of Pelleas and Etarre*, published the following year.

For this novel, if it can be called such, she arranged into a thematic sequence eight previously published stories and nine new ones. She intended their common theme to be the coming of spring and its meaning to two old lovers "in whom the joy and satisfaction of that companionship would be revivified with each birth of the new season."[4] In these stories Pelleas and Etarre, each seventy years old, reminisce about their long life together which has been tragically marked by their son's death and their loss of money, yet sustained by love. The old couple, always in perfect accord, find their greatest pleasure in assisting young lovers (thus the title of the book) in elopements, reunions, christenings, and the business of fostering bliss. The one character clearly emerging from all this old-time lavender is Nichola, a crotchety Italian cook-maid-factotum who has loyally served them ever since she got off the boat at twenty. Her presence, unfortunately, never sufficiently dominates to remove the pink-cloud atmosphere in what the New York *Tribune* (Oct. 5, 1907) called this "pretty book" appropriately dedicated to Mama and Papa Gale.

Swathed in sweetness and light, Zona Gale continued by these stories to make her small contribution to the lingering romanticism of the new century. Oblivious to the scientific, positivistic, and radical spirit which was replacing the waning antiquarianism of tradition, she wrote these literary samplers with no rebellion against the undercurrents. Unlike Howells, Henry James, and Edith Wharton, who recognized that a new middle class was displacing citizens of wealth and fashion, Zona Gale was content to write her little tales, certain she wanted nothing to do with literary realism or anything else shutting the door on sunshine.

Her decision to move back to Portage, where she knew her materials, saved her from complete literary inconsequence. She felt that staying in New York would finally impoverish her writing, for there she drew on no real-life sources. *Romance Island*, she said, was only "a feather from a flightless wing"; *Pelleas and Etarre* was hardly an improvement. In Portage would be new materials, a new identity, and, of course, her parents.

II

At first glance her Friendship Village stories, written in Portage, appear impossibly remote from the bustle of a new era. Nevertheless, Zona Gale intended in them to synthesize national disparities and to reveal a common denominator, a simple humanity, an essential federation, which undergirded America. The simple virtues of her Friendship Villagers represented the American character at its finest; the keynote to all her early work was the fundamental and intrinsic oneness of humanity, whether living in retired villages or great cities. "New York is simply a magnified Friendship Village," she said, and "folks are just folks, after all."[5] As Steinbeck's Preacher Casy might have added, each village soul is just a chunk of a bigger one. Zona Gale believed that Portage, Wisconsin, her Friendship Village, reflected in its pool all the people and all the stars. This was the substance of her Village stories which, for the next eleven years, she wrote with little variation.

In 1908 the first collection of twenty Village stories was published simply as *Friendship Village*. Nineteen more appeared the next year in *Friendship Village Love Stories*, nineteen in *When I Was A Little Girl* (1913), eleven in *Neighborhood Stories* (1914), and eighteen in *Peace in Friendship Village* (1919). In addition to these eighty-three stories, she wrote a Friendship Village novel entitled *Mothers to Men* (1911), a novelette, *Christmas* (1912), and a one-act play, *The Neighbors* (1914).

In all these works the same village characters reappear. The dominant figure is Calliope Marsh, sixty years old and shrewd, whose understanding of her village and whose splendid common sense identify her, one may suppose, with Eliza Beers Gale. Calliope—a mender of lace, a seller of extracts, and a music teacher—is unfailingly the quiet intelligence behind scenes. Neighbors easily confide in her and she, in turn, offers wise counsel. Mis' Amanda Toplady, Calliope's companion, is large, slow-moving, and amiable. Always the pacifist, she has little trouble quieting her husband, Timothy, who, like a cricket, loves to talk and always says "Blistering Benson of Cat's sake" when excited. Mis' Postmaster Sykes (Friendship Village women sometimes assume for their given name the employment, if distinguished, of their husbands) is the inveterate chairman of committees, the "leader," whose aimless earnestness is as tiresome as her husband's bombast. Mis' Holcomb is lean and unattractive, and so too is her husband, Eppleby. Abel Halsey, as a young itinerant minister, understands Human Problems and, with Calliope, is sensible about their alleviation. The Proudfits live on Friendship Hill, their large, hilltop house testifying to Alex Proudfit's genius in business and enabling the family to have the leisure of "long days in pretty rooms." Between the Proudfit house and the village, squats Cadoza's house, "one of the unblossoming, dark kind, and awful ramshackle"; it is the house Calliope always "sort of dreaded." Mis' Merriman, who calls herself Mis' Fire Chief after her deceased husband, flaunts her mourning as a reason for being considered first on all occasions: "She done her mourning like she done her house work—thorough." The roll lengthens: Jimmy Sturgis and Mis' Photographer Sturgis ("The Dead from Photos a Speciality"); the Embers; Dick Dasher, the train engineer; Peleg Bemus, the wood-cutter; Mis'

Mayor Uppers; Mis' Abigail Arnold who runs the Home Bakery and who had a loaf of bread carved on her husband's grave marker. "How alike we are," muses Calliope, "and I dunno but it means something, something big."

In her Preface to *Neighborhood Stories* Zona Gale explained that "on the whole, we are all friends." So why, Ruth Suckow asked, do intellectuals scoff at vignettes of small-town folks, such as those in Friendship Village, who came straight from the raw, pioneering life of early days.[6] Miss Suckow, herself a writer of American village life, insisted upon the virtue of "getting together" and claimed that the old sense of one big family fostered the development of American towns. Big "feeds," corn-husking, barn-raising, games, choir rehearsals, "visiting," committee meetings—all were infused with the family atmosphere; so why, she asked, do intellectuals with Gargantuan laughter and sophisticated tolerance regard these folks as philistines lacking both art and ideas? Miss Suckow thought that, in their snobbish flight from home-town people, satirists like Lewis, Mencken, Howe, and Wescott had lost the spirit of participation. To Zone Gale these common folks living in a small town, talking about the same things, and sharing the same days symbolized the spectacle of humanity. In her Friendship Village stories this idea is central.

Later when she, too, satirized these same little people, she never ceased marveling at the stuff of their cohesiveness. Writing in 1928, she explained that attention to Calliope Marsh and the other villagers illustrated her own interest in discovering the implications of daily, routine living. "Great drama *is* great implication,"[7] a notion expressed in her life-long refrain that life is something more than what we believe it to be. Tiny Friendship Villages, such as Calliope's, have their own character which, Zona Gale believed, revealed itself in kindness and brotherhood.

Zona Gale's accomplishment in these stories was little more than bringing romanticism to a middle western town. In *Miss Lulu Bett* and *Faint Perfume* few traces of romance remain. Before putting it aside, however, she strummed the same lyric about these townsfolk for eleven years. Friendship Village, with its fifteen hundred inhabitants, resembled the idealization of community life—neat, compact, moral, traditional. Its anti-intellectualism was a blessing, the people still remembering the old circuit-riders of a previous day who admonished that the thirst for knowledge drove Adam and Eve from Paradise. Sykes, Toplady, Proudfit, and their wives were free from such thirst. Zona Gale transformed superstition, pettiness, and bigotry into harmless and comic idiosyncracies. Instead of showing the folk as mundane and unlettered, as most of them were, she stressed their admirable gregariousness. She saw them as participants in the Middle Border saga, as distant kinsmen of Natty Bumppo, who, because he lived "in the very bosom of natur'," could interpret the mysteries of life and nature. Later western writers, taking their cue from Walt Whitman, reincarnated pioneers into mystics, dreamers, and prophets, and placed them in a veritable Garden. The archetype was, of course, Abraham Lincoln, who came unlettered from the Illinois prairies and who, by destiny, first achieved political prominence the same year Donati's comet appeared in the sky.

The Friendship Villagers are much more domesticated than these frontier heroes, but they inherit the same vision and voice the same hopes: "Let's dream—real far. Let's dream farther than gift-giving—and on up to wages—and mebbe a good deal farther than that. Let's dream the farthest that folks could go." Calliope and her neighbors share the conviction they are helping to shape a society, if not a race. They harbor a dim religiosity and, most importantly, acknowledge a solidarity binding them to the common experiences.

I don't know how well you know villages [Calliope says in *Neighborhood Stories*] but I hope you know anyhow one, because if you don't they's things to life that you don't know yet. Nice things. . . .

I was walking down Daphne Street pretty early, seeing everybody's breakfast fire smoke coming out of the kitchen chimney and hearing everybody's little boy splitting wood and whistling out in the chip pile, and smelling everybody's fried mush and warmed-up potatoes and griddle cakes come floating out sort of homely and old fashioned and comfortable, from the kitchen cook-stoves.

'Look at the Family,' I says to myself, 'sitting down to breakfast, all up and down the street.'

While in later novels Friendship Village loses both its name and character, in these stories its name corresponds to the quaint charm of Daphne Street. Consider why, she asked in her first story of the series, the villagers did not call it Main or Clark or Cook or Grand Street? She thought that, because of the five hundred elms and oaks in the village, Daphne perhaps did herself "take this way on the day of her flight." Along Daphne Street were the in-no-way incongruous businesses: the telegraph and cable office, the Commercial Travelers' House, the Abigail Arnold Home Bakery. Out at the end of it were Timothy Toplady's Enterprise Pickle Manufactory and Silas Sykes's Friendship Village Canning Industry. No matter that Skyes paid little David Beach ("a nice little soul") only two and a half dollars a week for shelling corn or that the Good Shepherd's Orphans Home and the Alice County poor-house never shut their doors. To Sykes "folks are rich, or medium, or poor" and "it's always been so." The important condition is always that the villagers live together, that each keeps his house clean and ordered, that each person sometimes hands out old clothes and toys to the needy, and that every citizen respects the cultural sentimentalities of home, church, and nation.

As would be expected, some readers did not appreciate Zona Gale's picture of these simple folk, "too sickeningly dear and precious."[8] Fannie Hurst, who was not notable as a realist, thought that the Village was a "china shop of quaint porcelains" full of "musty phrases that went out with the sweeter age." Those who know better, she wrote, "laugh behind the painted fan."[9] The New York *Sun* (Jan. 4, 1920) pointed out that for one to enjoy these stories "it is absolutely essential that you be sentimental" and "let fall a tear or two." On the other hand, numerous readers praised Zona Gale's lively sense of humor and her perception of folkways. The New York *Evening Post* (Oct. 21, 1914) thought her characters so full of sage philosophy that they had come from "the famous school at Concord." When reading her stories, another critic wrote, "we bask for a few pleasant hours in that exhilarating human sunshine that radiates straight from the heart of people who are real and true and big of soul."[10] Some reviewers compared Zona Gale with Jane Austen and Mrs. Elizabeth Gaskell. Of all the critical appraisals of the Friendship Village stories, Constance Rourke's review of *Peace in Friendship Village* shows the most careful reading.[11] Looking back over all the Village stories, she traced Calliope Marsh's growth from a rose-pink "dealer in maxims" to a "plain, downright village woman." "Rose Pink," the title of a story, is the popular color, Miss Rourke observed, that wraps "the flimsy manufactured episodes like masses of tissue paper and yards of ribbon." Later on, this color gradually changes to gray; and in *Peace in Friendship Village,* with which her review was immediately concerned, she noted that a few tales led away from contentment, the uplift was less assured, and the satire on civic clubs and philanthropy sharper.

It would be inaccurate to regard the Friendship Village stories as nothing more than literary Christmas cards. Behind all Zona Gale's peace on earth the reader detects a restlessness in her main character, Calliope, suggesting that this kindly soul, for one, is not convinced of the village's perfection. Silas Sykes and his fellow Rotarians may believe in the immutable laws of social stratification, but Calliope thinks society needs reform. She is too charitable to ascribe Sykes's conservatism to self-interest and exploitation, to laissez-faire and survival of the fittest. To her it is all a matter of education. If people learn what constitutes "humanhood," they will inevitably grow more magnanimous and, in turn, more cohesive. Then they will think in terms of everyone's sharing the good works of each.

Zona Gale's concept of good works was synonymous with civic improvements. Private virtue needed to be translated into public achievements. In her Preface to *Neighborhood Stories* she looked forward to a new "to-morrow" when community consciousness could reform every village and town. Her formula was simple. If the citizens could be taught to consider first the welfare of the community, then plan together the practical steps for reform, and finally work together to achieve it, there would be good reason to expect that every community following this procedure could boast of friendship.

Her suppositions in these stories are naïve, not so much regarding her method for social betterment but rather her confidence in the facility and ease which these reforms would occur. An increasing number of writers were challenging optimistic reformers with evidence that American democracy, founded upon the notion of individual rights, served only the negative function of allowing the fit the right to grow fitter and the unfit the right to die. Jacob Riis's *How the Other Half Lives* (1890) might better have been called How the Other Nine-Tenths Live.

Lincoln Steffens showed that what seemed the apotheosis of American civic development was, instead, *The Shame of the Cities* (1904). Books added to those of the celebrated muckrakers offered shocking evidence that friendship hardly described the American common tie.

Even so, Zona Gale's outlook was not hopelessly unsophisticated. Her dissatisfaction with the status quo compelled her to assert, again in the Preface to *Neighboring Stories,* that women must be freed from household drudgery; that a new liberalism must energize religion; that divorce should be applauded "when shame or faithlessness or disease or needless invalidism have attended marriage"; that puritan inhibitions have covered up far too much and that now it is to people's credit that they "mention openly things which in the old days we whispered or guessed at." These ideas, in their own way, indicated a good deal of social radicalism. It is necessary to remember that in the 1920's Zona Gale's reputation as an outspoken liberal and reformer left her Friendship Village stories all but forgotten. To notice the comfortable assumptions underlying them serves to emphasize the later dramatic awakening of her own social consciousness.

III

While writing her Friendship Village tales, Zona was comfortably situated with her parents in their new colonial house on Edgewater Street. From her back, second-floor study she looked upon the wide lawn sloping down to the river's edge. The Wisconsin River, at this point, spreads tranquilly out from beyond the giant elms and walnut trees which shaded her window. She left every autumn to visit New York where she placed stories with *The Delineator, Harper's Monthly, Everybody's, The Outlook,* and *The Woman's Home Companion.* Her closest friend among the editors was Charles Hanson Towne who joined *The Delineator* in 1910 and the following year, in a contest of short fiction which his magazine sponsored, awarded first prize of $2000 to Zona Gale for her piece, "The Ancient Dawn." As Towne explained in *Adventures in Editing* (1926), the first prize would have gone to a John Oskison if he had not exceeded the three-thousand-word limitation by three hundred. The second-best

story, Zona Gale's, became the first. With the money she thought
of following Towne's suggestion to go to Europe, but Mama
Gale's letter on January 12, 1912, begged her to "come on home."
Capitulating to this request, Zona Gale informed Towne that instead of going to Europe she was "going back home—[to] write a
better story."[12]

At this time she became active in the development of the
Wisconsin Dramatic Society, one of the earliest little-theater
movements in the country. Most of the plays emerging from the
group were one-acts, the best-known being Zona Gale's *The
Neighbors*. The Society's founder, Professor Thomas Dickinson
of the University of Wisconsin, had wanted Miss Gale to write a
play using the typical Friendship Village setting. "Write us a
simple scene," he asked, "wound around a single episode beating
with one human emotion taken from the single life of a village."
And end the play, he requested, "with just a little tear and a
smile." In less than a month Miss Gale sent the completed manuscript to Dickinson who immediately answered, "The play does.
Have just read it with delight. We shall produce it this spring."[13]

Zona Gale's regional themes and her interest in community development comprise the main business in the play which, five
years later, Professor A. M. Drummond of Cornell University
asked to use for his Cornell Dramatic Club at the New York State
Fair. She allowed Drummond to produce the play without paying
her a royalty fee provided that for every performance he promised
to plant a tree in the community. "And if the producers wish to
give really good measure for the use of the play," she wrote,
"it is recommended that they conclude the evening with a community gathering, with community singing and dancing, and a
discussion of the things which their community needs."[14]

Her civic interests matched her literary vigor. Believing that
little towns should develop an identity of their own, she wrote a
pamphlet in 1913 for the American Civic Association. Entitled
"Civic Improvement in the Little Towns," it outlined ways
local committees could work to enhance their towns. The twenty-
six-page pamphlet actually set down the framework for her
fictional treatment of the same issues. In it she asserted that the
problem of educating citizens to understand their corporate responsibility rested upon the three-fold theory that (1) the con-

servation of physical and moral life is largely economic, (2) that there are practical ways of applying this understanding to the present and future towns, and (3) that such application could be accomplished with "exceedingly little money." Clubs, especially women's clubs, might study such topics as gardens, playgrounds, public fountains, health, conservation, schools, and sanitation. She suggested ways for getting club constitutions written and standing committees organized. Using Portage as her example, she recommended the formation of such committees as: Education Committee, Children's Auxiliary Committee, Streets and Alleys Committee, Rest-Room Committee, Charity Co-Ordination Committee, Public Buildings and Recreations Committee, Sanitation Committee, Medical and Dental Inspection Committee, Garbage Collection Committee. Her abiding rationale was the virtue of public solidarity. She believed in committees. Alien to her and to her fictional characters in Friendship Village is the private search for both independence and meaning apart from society. True to her name, it is Calliope who beautifully voices the over-ruling sentiment: "Oh, deep inside us all ain't there something that says, I ain't you, nor you, nor you, nor five thousand of you. I'm all of you. I'm one."

Writers today have turned away from the easily ordered unity of man, nature, and God. After giving their readers *A Brave New World* and *1984,* they have made it nearly impossible for anyone ever to create another Utopia without irony. Scars are too deep for readers to take seriously such a work as B. F. Skinner's recent *Walden Two,* which describes a future Friendship Village where sociologists will isolate, correlate, and regulate their subjects' responses and thus create a new paradise free from serpents. Instead, serious writers have journeyed into the private world to discover what defies scientific regulation and to reconsider the meaning of such tarnished words as "expiation" and "grace." To them psychological and eschatological coherence is fragile. One squirms at the innocence in Zona Gale's blithe assumptions. One wishes to confront her with the screams of Roderick Usher or the maniacal laughter of Ethan Brand. She had yet to discover the terror compacted into those nineteenth-century American symbols of the raven, the white whale, and the scarlet letter. Those who today envision a Walden Two have not made the discovery either.

IV

To describe Zona Gale's eighty-three Friendship Village stories one can use the metaphor of concentric circles. In the common center is a governing principle, given maternal attributes, which radiates out through all the surrounding circles. The tales collected in *When I Was A Little Girl,* fanciful as they are, particularly illustrate that closest to this maternal center are children. In "Earth Mother," for example, an orphaned child is adopted by a woman who intones that we are all in someone's lap. The child in "The Great Black House" remembers wildly awaking one night fearful that her mother could no longer recognize her; she is comforted by her mother's words, "You are mine." There is no intimation here that the center cannot hold. Her tales, paeans of optimism, affirm a coalescing deity which impels and beautifies all that surrounds it.

Circling the center is the domestic household, one of her principal interests in these stories. One can think of few authors who insist so interminably on romanticizing the routine life of Washday, Ironday, Mend-day, Bakeday, Freeday, Scrubday, and Sunday. In later works she admits, with vehemence, that domestic work is downright drudgery, especially if it interferes with a woman's participation in civic affairs. Nevertheless, the home remains a sanctuary and the mother its center. Homemaking ennobles each member of the family; the routines resemble rituals. Planting the garden, making preserves, knitting rag rugs, bustling for company, dressing a dead child in grave clothes—all are meaningful acts. Contrary to T. S. Eliot's Hollow Men, the Friendship Villagers believe that shapes have form; shades, color; gestures, motion. It is true that Mis' Amanda Toplady or Mis' Fire Chief Merriman see little beyond their busy-work, but Calliope Marsh lives nearby to tell them about it. Calliope is the one who in "The Time Has Come" (*Neighborhood Stories*) describes a family as a "household of love," each member seeking to cultivate, as in "The Tea Party" (*Friendship Village*), a *"savoir faire* of the heart instead of the head."

The same familial harmony extends to the community. Zona Gale is not poking fun at the conscientious village ladies whose Friendship Married Ladies' Cemetery Improvement Sodality attends to such urgent matters as a new iron fence around the cemetery or a plan for more efficient garbage collection. In Friendship Village "the modern spirit," akin to progress, manifests itself in civic improvements; therefore, an invitation to help "advance the town" would read: "Will all them that's interested in seeing Friendship Village made as much a town as it could be, for all of us and for the children of all of us, meet together in Post-Office Hall to-morrow night, at 7 o'clock, to talk over if we're doing it as good as we could" ("The Biggest Business," *Neighborhood Stories*). The minutes from such a meeting would read: "A meeting of citizens of Friendship Village was held, ..., in Post-Office Hall, for the purpose of organizing a society to do nice things for folks. . . . A number of ways was thought of for going to work. Things that had ought to be done was talked over. It was decided to hold monthly meetings. Meeting adjourned" ("Exit Charity," *Neighborhood Stories*). The question raised at every meeting is inevitably Calliope's: "What shall we *do* to make it [the Village] whole?" Important as Benefits, Auxiliaries, Ladies' Aid, and the Cemetery Improvement Sodality may be in beautifying the town, the greater good is in unifying it. Of the ladies' planting geraniums around the depot Calliope says, with her own italics, "*We was one person.*"

The fact that Zona Gale so conveniently reconciles differences among the villagers raises questions about both her understanding and her artistic integrity. Sentimentality obscures her observation, justifying the complaint of many critics who thought Zona Gale was merely going the way of popular magazine writers, making money out of a stupid optimism, preaching an all's-right-with-the-world doctrine, when her common sense must have told her often enough that all was not right."[15] More to the point is that as long as Zona Gale entertained the illusion that a Romance Island or a Friendship Village might exist, she felt justified in creating it in her fiction. When the time came for this illusion to be shattered, exposing the desolation of reality, she then wrote much differently.

V

Five years separated *Neighborhood Stories* and *Peace in Friendship Village* (1919), her last volume of village tales. During this interval Zona Gale wrote three novels: *Heart's Kindred* (1915), a wild plea for pacifism; *A Daughter of the Morning*

(1917), an economic novel faintly resembling Howells' later ones; and *Birth* (1918), unquestionably her first work of literary distinction. Her outlook had now begun to change; her style grew more severe, her themes more socially relevant. "The Story of Jeffro," published in *Everybody's Magazine* in 1915, marks this turning-point. Exposing the villagers' hypocrisy in their treatment of Jeffro, a Jew, she leaves no room for sentimentality. In the same year she submitted a story to the *Atlantic Monthly* called "The Reception Surprise"; its theme announces the need for social equality between whites and blacks. Ellery Sedgwick, the *Atlantic* editor, would have none of it.[16] The same story had earlier stirred up a storm at *Everybody's Magazine,* Gilman Hall explaining to her that she was "a little too far ahead in this story."[17]

Her daughter's interests in socialism frightened Mama Gale; she regarded labor strikers as ragged gangs unable to govern anything, even themselves. Furthermore, she urged her daughter to have nothing to do with the National Suffrage Movement, advising her: "I would let that mess of women *alone*."[18] But Zona Gale would not be distracted. During World War I and the decade following, her work for liberal reforms commanded wide attention and respect. Hamlin Garland's judgment was typical: "She is a great little woman."[19]

Small wonder, then, that Constance Rourke noticed a difference in Zona Gale's last volume of Village stories, *Peace in Friendship Village,* when it appeared in 1919. The New York *Sun* (Jan. 4, 1920), failing to notice this difference, merely sighed that "Zona Gale has gone back to Friendship Village"; that "there are those who welcomed her with hands and singing, but we were not among them"; and that Calliope is still "a disgustingly good soul." The difference lay in the tone as well as subject matter. The Sykes and Topladys, Mis' Merriman, and the Holcombs are more contentious, more reluctant to listen to Calliope. Bigotry and meanness, now more deeply rooted, cannot be mollified by bringing people together to plant geraniums. The unity supposedly centered in every village and in every family now becomes crusty provincialism, hostile to every outsider. When, for example, in the story "Dream" Mis' Sykes learns that the new neighbors moving into the Oldmoxon House are colored, she exclaims to Calliope about Mis' Fernandez, "My gracious,

ZONA GALE

ain't you got no sense of fitness to you. Ain't she black?" Silas
Sykes croaks that "they're different by nature" and resolves to
kick them out; he pays no attention to Calliope's news that the
husband is a college professor and that Mis' Fernandez is a college graduate. "Oh, God," Calliope prayerfully whispers, "we
here in America got up a terrible question for you to help us
settle, didn't we? Well, *help* us! And help us to see, whatever's
the way to settle anything, that giving the cold shoulder and the
uplifted nose to any of the creatures you've made ain't the way
to settle *nothing*. Amen."

This sentiment piqued the townspeople of Portage as much
as Zona Gale's stand on pacifism did. Several stories in *Peace in
Friendship Village* make it clear that her view of the war included
no resentment toward the German people but only against the
group standing for militarism and autocracy. "The Feast of
Nations" and "The Cable" paid tribute to all nations whose blood
flowed in battle. Her international sympathy plus her refusal to
buy national Liberty Bonds aroused angry words from Portage
citizens who, despite their long friendship with her, nodded
approvingly when the Secret Service occasionally looked in on her
activities. (On one occasion her father satisfied the investigators
by showing some bonds purchased in her name and then later
confessed to her that he had bought them, without her knowledge, for just such eventualities.) "When the Hero Came Home"
broadly ridiculed the superpatriots—specifically the D.A.R.'s
and the G.A.R.'s in Friendship Village—who spoke about "the
glories of war" when they welcomed back the men, some dis-
figured beyond recognition. In her most eloquent moment,
Calliope shouts above the orators gathered at the depot: "The
glories of war! You do not know what you say! I tell you that I
have seen mad dogs, mad beasts of prey—but I do not know
what it is they do. The glories of war! Oh, my God, does nobody
know that we are all mad together?"

These are strange words to hear in Friendship Village. They
are ominously echoed by Mis' Amanda Toplady who, when
noticing how quickly Silas Sykes jumps to his feet when the
"Star Spangled Banner" is played, whispers to Calliope: "When-
ever a man gets up so *awful* sudden when one of his country's
airs is played, I always think I'd just love to look into his business
life, and make perfectly sure that he ain't a-making money in

ways that ain't patriotic to his country, nor a credit to his citizen-ship—in the real sense." Obviously Zona Gale had come a long way from her first Village stories in 1908. The climax came when she included in this last volume "The Story of Jeffro," considered later by editor Gilman Hall as "one of the best stories we have published in *Everybody's* in recent years."[20]

Her Prologue to the story struck a new note to her fiction which, with *Birth* and *Miss Lulu Bett* (1920), secured her position among America's literary realists.

> When I have told this story of Jeffro, the alien [she wrote], some one has always said: "Yes, but there's another side to that. They aren't all Jeffros.'
>
> When stories are told of American gentleness, childlike faith, sensitiveness to duty, love of freedom, I do not remember to have heard any one rejoin: "Yes, but Americans are not all like that."
>
> So I wonder why this comment should be made about Jeffro.

Jeffro had come to America with his eight-year-old son to save enough money to bring the rest of the family over. Though Friendship Villagers insisted on calling him "that Jew peddler," he strongly believed that America stood for freedom and he was happy making and selling toys. Cold winter snows, however, made him realize that his little house, which had partially burned one autumn night, could not be adequately heated for his little boy. The roof was decayed, windows shrunken, and the floor drafty from all directions. He decided to leave his son with neighbors, deposit his summer savings of thirty-seven dollars in the village bank, and take a job as a coal miner in the next state. No one heard from him all winter. In the spring he returned, almost starved and still weak after recovering from a bullet wound in his shoulder. That was the spring, Calliope remembers, that the bank closed and the panic was "just another name for somebody's greed, dressed up becoming as Conditions." Upon his return Jeffro told his bewildering story to Calliope:

> "Ve vere standing there outside the Angel mine," he said, "to see that nobody vent to vork and spoiled our hopes ven somebody cried out: 'The soldiers!' Many of the men ran—I did not know why. Here was some of the United States army. I had never seen any of the army before. . . . I stood bowing. My

heart felt good. They had come to help us then—free! And then somebody cried, 'He's one of the damned, disorderly picketers. Arrest him!' And they did; and nothing I could say vould make them understand."

Jeffro explained to Calliope that he had only wanted to earn his bread. Instead, he had been shot in the shoulder by an American soldier. Hopefully, he confided to her, "To-morrow I vill get out from the bank my money—I have not touched that—and send to her vat I have." When told that the bank had failed, Jeffro stood dazed. "Then this too can happen in America. And the things I see all winter—the soldiers to shoot you down?"

Zona Gale was now like a metal spring tightened and ready to lash out only to recoil and lash out again and again. Her Jeffro story was just the beginning. Her fight to be heard, especially in Wisconsin, on matters of political, social, and educational reform counterpointed her insistence that antifeminine prejudices imposed by the conventional barriers of tradition be broken down. To the tune of William James's pragmatism and Thorstein Veblen's economics and to the chorus of women dissenters— Dorothy Canfield Fisher, Mary Austin, Susan Glaspell, Jane Addams, Anne Douglas Sedgwick, Edith Wharton—Zona Gale added her highly articulate voice.

Strangely enough, she did not dispose of the sentiments which sweetened her earlier Friendship Village stories. They ran too deeply for that. Her full-sized novel *Mothers to Men,* the novelette *Christmas,* and the play *The Neighbors*—all written with familiar saccharinity—had added even more bulk to her already surfeited storehouse of romance, love, and friendship. Each work merely amplified the basic themes of her stories: *Mothers to Men* and *Christmas* deal with the mysteriously centripetal manner by which nature, fecund and maternal, unifies all people; and *The Neighbors* dramatizes the vicissitudes of young lovers, one a grocery boy and the other a housemaid. But for much of her forthcoming work, she did free herself from her rosy sentiments. In returning to them later, she transformed them into something far more mature, substantial, and provocative.

CHAPTER 3

Social Action and Politics

I

REMOTE AS PORTAGE WAS, Zona Gale plunged into state and national issues with a vigor probably unmatched by any other woman writer of her day. For example, when in 1915 the Wisconsin Senate was divided by a narrow margin, State Senator George Standenmeyer paid weekly visits to Miss Gale's home to ask her advice about pending legislation. At the end of each legislative week she would receive from Charles McCarthy, the state reference librarian in Madison, a special-delivery letter analyzing the legislative events of the preceding week. The result was that the senator marveled at the novelist's wide knowledge of political matters, and on many bills he voted according to her recommendations. When his vote broke a tie, as it frequently did, she justifiably claimed a decisive influence on the legislation.[1]

Literature was only one of her many interests. It was, of course, her dominant one, but after her return to quiet Portage she awakened to others. In New York she had been only dimly aware of the social scene: the preventable bad living and working conditions, the comfort and complacence of the few and the misery of the many. Years later she explained to Robert M. La Follette, Jr., that political Progressivism to her at that time was only "a program of a lot of malcontents—pestilent fellows!"[2] She had had little concern for the Progressives' efforts toward labor and health legislation, child welfare, public ownership of utilities, women suffrage, and improvement of state institutions. Then one day after her return to Portage she picked up a copy of *La Follette's Magazine* (started in 1909 as the unofficial organ of the insurgent, La Follette-led Republicans). She was amazed to find there, a page of material on the very matters whose urgency had only slowly begun to attract her. In his same letter to Robert La Follette, Jr., she told of reading on, number after number, and of realizing that here was a fundamental movement whose principles placed human welfare above property, that here was a political party—Progressivism—which sought to bring government to the people by eliminating corruption and special privilege. It all was, she said, "a revelation." "And I began to watch that small group that went year after year to the Republican National Conventions, presenting their platforms to audiences that laughed & hissed & called them socialists. . . . I saw that this was not only a political movement, but the recognition of fundamental issues which business administrations had all but ignored—issues which were veritably issues of life, of human welfare, of human growth." She called this personal record "a kind of ABC statement" of her new social conscience.

In time this expanding social and political awareness changed her fiction from the insipid romanticism of her Friendship Village stories to first-rate realism. Moreover, it fired her energies in a host of non-literary activities. Not only did she continually stump for "Fighting Bob" La Follette, Sr., and work tirelessly with him for Progressive legislation in Wisconsin, but she also turned her attention to such famous social movements of the day as pacifism, women's rights and suffrage, labor conditions, social welfare, and education. So important were these activities to her that they deserve elaboration even apart from their influence upon her literary work. Seen in this way, they reveal facets of Zona Gale's life which otherwise might be obscured by the erroneous notion that she was merely a spinner of literary lace, shielded in idyllic Portage from contemporary realities.

II

Until her death in 1938 Zona Gale's activities usually related to the fact that she was a reformist, her femininity cloaking with silk a hard-bitten tenacity always gracious but always firm. Her poignant consciousness of home and community life extended to state, national, and international life, and it was structured on the premise that a person's work must be cooperative. This sense, "not of *me, working,* but of *the people, working* [italics hers]"[3] illumined her social message.

This type of social evangelism led to sobering questions. She had serious misgivings about economic competition as a system which allowed for little if any cooperativeness. She contended that social action had to be infused with socially relevant religious principles if it hoped to meet the contemporary challenges of war, inequalities, poverty, corruption, and competitive ruthlessness. This viewpoint brought her together with many American intellectuals, including Walter Rauschenbush, who popularized the term Social Gospel through such books as *Christianity and the Social Crisis* (1907) and *Social Principles of Jesus* (1916). A professor of church history at the Rochester Theological Seminary, he challenged reformers to build human society upon religious concepts. Zona Gale devoured Rauschenbush's books. Immediately after his *Theology for the Social Gospel* appeared in 1918, she told him that his book "links" social and religious consciousness.[4]

She equated a social wrong with sin, which she defined as anything which prevents or delays growth in body, mind, and spirit. Rauschenbush in his 1918 book used the word "sin" in terms of social forces which "enervate and submerge." He argued along with other social gospelers like John R. Commons, Frances Willard, and Hamlin Garland that social sins too often had been side-stepped by an orthodox theology which failed to touch the secular. He maintained that a moral judgment must expose these sins. In like manner, Zona Gale declared that disease, poverty, all working conditions which cramp and inhibit growth, the use of child labor, and war, were "wrong."

All wrongs against the free spirit in man she called antisocial or sinful. She was not beguiled by the conservatives' argument that disease was a divine visitation, and that anyone who tried to stamp it out violated divine law; or that poverty, as incurable as certain fevers, was to be accepted as a providential edict requiring certain human beings to be "tested." She saw that the so-called natural law of anarchic privilege justifying the rise of the strong and the decline of the weak belied both the idealistic Declaration of Independence and the Christian Gospels. Rather than depending upon the blind forces of strength, greed, or fate to determine those persons who would survive, Progressive intellectuals, including Zona Gale, believed that intelligent cooperativeness, necessitating legislative regulations, could establish a social climate in which each person's rights were upheld and his own potential realized.

Her concern for social reform led her down many avenues, some of them odd and unlikely and, perhaps, bearing little connection with customary reform. For instance, she took up gentle cudgels against trappers who inhumanely allowed their fur-bearing animals to suffer in traps before dying. Though she hardly knew how to cook, she believed that for healthy growth one should not eat preserved fruits and jellies, white sugar, white flour, vinegar, heavy desserts, egg whites, salt after forty, and meat. Child discipline, she thought, should "unfold" the child by means of wise cooperation instead of quick and excited prohibitions. Hopes to curb excessive smoking among students led her, as a regent of the University of Wisconsin, to favor continued prohibition of tobacco advertising in the student newspaper, the *Daily Cardinal*.

Other interests were less bizarre. She favored the Eighteenth Amendment which prohibited the manufacture and sale of intoxicating liquors. After its adoption in January, 1920, she opposed La Follette's wet plank in the Progressive platform of 1924. Reasons for her opposition stemmed from an attitude condemning as wrong anything thwarting personal growth. Because, she argued, "*any amount* [of alcohol] *puts some of the brain to sleep* [italics hers],"[5] she supported the Volstead Act which, following on the heels of the Eighteenth Amendment, defined an intoxicating drink as one having as much as one-half of one percent alcohol. She was confident that legislated prohibition would prove that people are willing to subordinate their own tastes for the good of the group. (The extent of their cooperativeness was best measured by the increased bootlegging and national crime waves, centered in Chicago, only a four-hour train ride from Portage!) She gave generous credit to Frances Willard as one who "dared anything" for Prohibition and for the establishment of the Woman's Christian Temperance Union; its headquarters were in "dry" Evanston, now adjacent to Northwestern University, where Miss Willard served as its first Dean of Women. Zona Gale described her as "a hard-headed wise young woman with a grand social spirit" whose aim to "make the world more homelike" was exactly like her own.[6]

In establishing a more homelike world Zona Gale aligned herself with causes often repudiated by "homey," middle-class citizens. In August, 1927, she joined the "Save Sacco and

Vanzetti!" movement, organized to save Nicola Sacco, a shoe-maker, and Bartolomeo Vanzetti, a fish peddler, from execution on a charge of murdering in April, 1920, the paymaster and a guard of a Massachusetts shoe factory. Many American intellectuals charged that because the condemned men were radicals as well as aliens, the jury's finding them guilty displayed obvious racial, political, and economic prejudice. The Sacco-Vanzetti Defense Committee in Boston supervised picket lines set up to protest the execution scheduled for August 22. Many writers—including John Dos Passos, Michael Gold, Edna St. Vincent Millay, Dorothy Parker, Katherine Anne Porter—joined the lines and then were promptly arrested despite their constitutional right of free assembly. In desperation a Citizens' National Committee for Sacco and Vanzetti, formed by Robert Morss Lovett, Glenn Frank, and David Starr Jordan, appealed to the federal government to re-examine the evidence of the case. A telegram sent to President Coolidge ineffectually urged a stay of execution. Zona Gale signed this telegram, as did other literary figures: Fannie Hurst, Upton Sinclair, Horace Liveright, Vida Scudder, Ida M. Tarbell, John Dos Passos, Joseph Wood Krutch, Carl Van Doren, Katherine Anne Porter, Floyd Dell.[7]

She supported Louis Adamic's Foreign Language Information Service and his efforts to foster interracial tolerance and integration. As a member of the American Civil Liberties Union, she strongly objected to proposed New York state legislation in 1924 requiring a school teacher to take a loyalty oath. She expressed surprise to playwright Sidney Howard that "anybody should think such a law necessary, or should even think of it at all."[8] When the South Dakota legislature attempted to reinstate capital punishment in 1927, she argued that "legalizing murder" as a penalty for crime would recall Inquisition days when the rack and thumbscrew, even drawing and quartering, were considered by good respectable citizens to be necessary in the preservation of law and order.[9]

"Sitting out there in Wisconsin," as Elmer Rice laconically put it,[10] she supported such varied groups as: The Presbyterian Church, the Presbyterian Pension Board, American Woman's Hospital, Children's Aid Society, Wisconsin Temperance Education Association, American Library Association, Friends of Native Landscapes, Salvation Army, Emergency Peace Campaign, Wisconsin Society for the Friendless, Society for the Advancement of Colored People, Woman's Peace Union, Boys' Conservation Bureau, League to Abolish Capital Punishment, Authors League, Woman's International League for Peace and Freedom, Volunteers of America. All these interests involved her in heavy correspondence, frequent speech-making, compliance with magazine editors requesting articles, and considerable financial outlay.

Her desire to help young writers was yet another part of her busy career. A portion of her voluminous mail consisted of letters from well-meaning students and hopeless matrons requesting guidance with their writing problems. Each of these neophytes she answered with tact and sincerity. She also assisted more promising writers. When Glenway Wescott, then a young Wisconsin novelist, published *The Grandmothers* (1927), she tried her best to influence Carl Van Doren and the Literary Guild Board to sponsor it. She generously encouraged her Portage neighbor, Margery Latimer, only to receive curt repudiation later from novelist Latimer who in *We Are Incredible* and *Guardian Angel* intended obvious criticism of Zona Gale's supposedly excessive domination. Miss Gale recognized the accusation and quietly answered it in one of her own later novels, *Borgia* (1929), in which Marfa Manchester serves as the fictional counterpart to Latimer. Of notable importance in her effort to help young writers was her Zona Gale Scholarship for University of Wisconsin students who showed promise. She repeatedly stated that the chief thing to be done for anyone with creative ability was to let him alone; consequently, the scholarship stipulated only that the recipient make good grades in whatever he selected to study. Many students, including Margery Latimer, Eliseo Vivas, and Mark Schorer, received the scholarship, which paid a monthly sum of fifty dollars throughout one year. Professor Schorer, in 1929 a senior at Madison, remembers that "the bounty then seemed so extraordinary."[11]

III

Amid all this criss-cross of activity a few key public issues riveted her attention. One of these was pacifism. Preceding World War I, movements for world peace attained lofty heights. Peacemakers were drawing inspiration from eighteenth-century enlightenment and nineteenth-century liberalism, from the Monroe Doctrine, and from William Jennings Bryan's leadership in Progressive politics. Their manifest mission was to convince the world that America marched in the vanguard of all peace crusades. In 1910 Edward Ginn, the textbook publisher, organized the World Peace Foundation; the same year Andrew Carnegie gave ten million dollars to the Carnegie Endowment for International Peace. Following in rapid succession came the Women's Peace Party led by Jane Addams and Carrie Chapman Catt, the National Peace Council, the American Truth Society, the Friends of Peace, the Emergency Peace Federation, and similar organizations. President Woodrow Wilson was himself an inspired pacifist until, finally, he succeeded in establishing an all-important ideological justification for entering the war. Wisconsin's Senator Robert La Follette's pacifism filled the pages of *La Follette's Magazine*, while his protest against national conscription came in his refusal to march with the conscripts in their first Washington parade.

Back in Wisconsin the super-patriotic Dane County Defense Committee in Madison moved quickly to censure La Follette and to force the resignation of those members who denounced the committee's action against him. Forty miles away in Portage Zona Gale began work on her own statement, published in 1915 as *Heart's Kindred* and dedicated "to those who obey the Sixth Commandment."

This novel ruffled some excitement among reviewers.[12] What they read was a story about a besotted miner in California who inexplicably attracts Lory Moor, a woman considerably more civilized. Her role is to redirect his monomania from war to peace and then to brotherhood. Admittedly Lory's task will not be easy, for the miner's fixation on killing birds, like young Popeye's in Faulkner's *Sanctuary*, suggests his uncontrollable propensity for destroying life. His resolve to "join up" takes him to Chicago where, with Lory, he attends a mass meeting held to decide the question, "What is America to do in the present crisis?" Consensus favors those who want war; and, in an hysterical demonstration, the packed human mass "moved like maggots" in their chant, "To war . . . war . . . war!" Lory sobs, "They're voting to kill folks—oh my God!"; the unconverted California miner growls, "It's grand! It's—it's grand. . . ." His conversion, however, is not long delayed. At the bedside of his dying father he suddenly envisions a terrifying scene: battlefields and piles of dead soldiers. Breaking through his mania for war is the momentary consciousness that "he himself was God and he had been killing men." This Whitmanesque vision leads to Zona Gale's favorite refrain, this time applying to the miner's joyful realization that "his life was something other than that which he had believed it to be."

Zona Gale intended the novel as propaganda. The mixture, as might be expected, impaired the effectiveness of both the art and the propaganda. Its sermonizing spelled death to skillful handling of character and plot. The whole thing was bizarre. Nevertheless, its chief aim as feminine peace propaganda appealed to many, most notably to Jane Addams who read the book in manuscript and considered it nearly faultless. Her only suggestion for strengthening the novel's impact was that Zona Gale should intensify "the sense of difficulty which women in the warring nations feel when they are obliged to protest."[13]

This obligation to protest accounts for Zona Gale's active participation in the Woman's Peace Party. She found a publisher in John Haynes Holmes, editor of *Unity*, for such pacifistic articles as "Outlaw War Now!" (Oct. 18, 1923) and "The Crime of the Ages" (May 15, 1924). She urged that a plank outlawing war be included in every political party's platform. To swing the pendulum further away from war psychology, she called for toy manufacturers to discontinue making toy soldiers and guns. She spoke out against military training in colleges and universities; on one occasion in 1935 she refused an invitation to be a patroness at Ripon College's military ball because she opposed departments of military science in colleges and universities. The next year when asked to help sponsor a plan to send men and women to participate in the Spanish Civil War, she flatly refused on the grounds that fighting accomplished nothing.

Underlying all these protests against militarism was her steadfast belief that the rules of life prohibited war. She believed that man's inherent goodness would establish peaceful human relationships, a notion which accorded with the basic assumption most Progressives held, namely, that life was a process in which reason, good nature, and humane practices constituted the fundamental rules, to be translated into reform legislation including even the abolition of war.

Despite the gathering signs of war in the 1930's, Zona Gale's faith in human enlightenment assured her that peaceful means would be found to settle international differences. Her death in December, 1938, saved her from the terribly contrary fact. In one of her last public statements she told how she sighed with relief at the outcome of the Munich conference in September of the same year. She believed that England's Prime Minister Neville Chamberlain had averted war by peaceful counsel and conciliation. She interpreted President Franklin Roosevelt's international letters urging peace as a persuasive voice of friendliness and of reason. She died thinking that the achievement of a peace by words instead of by bloodshed was the triumph of her time. The abyss which soon opened still separates Zona Gale from today's readers.

A second key issue concerned women's rights. Zona Gale moved on the tide which started in 1792 when Mary Wollstonecraft argued in "The Vindication of the Rights of Women" that if women were freed from domestic impediments and social limitations they would demonstrate impressive capabilities. In 1844 Margaret Fuller used the same argument in "Woman in the Nineteenth Century," probably the first feminist tract in America. The presuppositions, of course, were that women, as rational and worthy individuals, ought to be afforded outlets for their intellectual and emotional life.

Women wanted to get off the domestic treadmill, falsely romanticized by so many men. They wanted to enter the universities and then the professions. Mary Austin wrote that they wanted to go "into intellectual life as a man goes" and expect the same return "in money and honor."[14] Self-determination in sexual relations, in marriage, in employment and career, in education, in politics—this was the swelling movement which reached a smashingly successful climax in 1920 with the Nineteenth Amendment granting women suffrage. With this victory, symbolically liberating women, Zona Gale believed they would no longer accept the humdrum life of their mothers whose marriages were flawed by a routine the new generation would not tolerate.

Many separate influences combined to liberate women. The early Chautauqua circles led to widespread public education, day and night schools for ambitious young women, women's club movements, and coeducational state universities. Thousands of women were sent on to buy books, hold meetings, take examinations, exhibit awards, and frame diplomas. At the same time a domestic revolution was bringing into the home new conveniences—improved lighting, inside plumbing, furnaces, sewing machines—which gave women more leisure time for outside affairs. Growth of women's organizations signalized the more important fact that by 1900 there were over five thousand college and professional women in the United States. From these educational and domestic changes came what Zona Gale called the loss of "certain reticences." The social atmosphere reduced "women-worship," allowing the individual woman other justifications for her existence than merely her condition as, say, a virgin, a wife, or a mother. Less than a year before she died Zona Gale took the trouble to write to the Mother's Day Foundation in New York objecting to the sentimental use of Whistler's mother in connection with Mother's Day observances. Far more important were a woman's capacities as a friend, a leader, or a worker. For as Chicago's Floyd Dell once quipped, "Even an oyster can be a mother."

The need, then, was for women to learn to use leisure time. Zona Gale feared the consequences if emancipation degenerated into little circles of ladies merely coming together for bridge, tea, golf, and shows. She warned that, if liberated women look down on hard work and fail to accept their intellectual and social obligations, "one more dream of democracy will have been delayed."[15]

Emancipation was not for idleness and self-indulgence but rather for cooperative work. In Miss Gale's opinion the women best exemplifying this spirit were the Hull House group at 800 South Halstad Street. Working among the inarticulate and impoverished immigrant masses in Chicago's West Side, these university-trained women helped the European newcomers adjust to their difficult, new life. This meant, for example, teaching them English, helping them learn occupational and domestic skills, opening playgrounds for their children, and establishing public health services. Zona Gale unreservedly asserted that the "great ladies" of Chicago were those at Hull House: Jane Addams, Ellen Gates Starr, Mary E. McDowell, Grace Abbott, Sophonsiba P. Breckenridge, Louise DeKoven Bowen, Mary Robert Smith—not idlers in expensive clothes and jewels but those who "*have given their lives* to others [italics hers]."[16] She singled out other Chicago women: Julia C. Lathrop, who led in reforms for almshouses and insane asylums and who became the first head of the Children's Bureau in Washington, D.C.; Florence Kelley, instrumental in Illinois factory legislation; Dr. Alice Hamilton, who worked first at Hull House and then devoted herself to investigating and preventing industrial diseases. Revered above all the others was Jane Addams—the founder of Hull House, a pacifist, President of the Woman's League for Peace and Freedom, friend of La Follette and member of the Progressive party, and recipient of the first honorary degree awarded to a social worker by the University of Wisconsin. From the time Zona Gale first met Jane Addams as a Milwaukee newspaper reporter, she regarded her as a model of womanhood, possessing a brooding awareness of the facts of life and working to mollify their sting.

Ironically, women's rights did not follow emancipation if, indeed, one could call the seven and a half million women employed in 1910 "emancipated." Their average workday was ten hours, their weekly salary five dollars. Economic survival more than desire for freedom drove them from their kitchens. The majority of them found jobs in industry, a lesser number in teaching, selling, and clerical work. Discrimination against them in nearly every occupation, and especially in industry, led in the 1880's to Working Girls clubs and to widespread women membership in the Knights of Labor. In 1892 the American Federation of Labor appointed a woman organizer, Mary E. Kenny of Boston, to help combat intolerable factory conditions. Subjected to fire hazards, absence of sanitation, dangerous machinery, windows nailed shut, little light, and merciless foremen, women in the garment trades organized the International Ladies Garment Workers Union in 1900. Two years later Mary Kenny and Leonora O'Reilly founded the powerful Women's Trade Union League which in 1909-10 supplied pickets for the shirtwaist makers' strike in New York and Philadelphia, which was waged against Leiserson Company and the Triangle Shirtwaist Company for thirteen agonizing weeks in the middle of winter. Despite police assaults and adverse court rulings, the League aided women strikers wherever summoned, its branch in Chicago headed by Mary McDowell and well-known Hull House workers Ellen Gates Starr and Sophonsiba Breckenridge. The next year, thirty years after the first women joined the Knights of Labor, the demand of women's rights in industry rose to a thunder when on March 25, 1911, 146 working women lost their lives in the Triangle Shirtwaist Company fire. The nation was shocked to learn that the company had barred stairways to prevent the women from walking out on strike. Women not trapped in the holocaust jumped to their deaths on the pavement below.

In *A Daughter of the Morning* (1917) Cosma Wakely is the first of many Zona Gale heroines who escapes intolerable village entrapment only to discover in the big city that these bewildering industrial conditions are worse than anything she left behind. Friendship Village in this novel is no longer the peaceful haven; renamed Katytown, it now confines twenty-year-old Cossy to nagging parents and the stupid courting of Luke, the local bumpkin. Like Mamie in Carl Sandburg's *Chicago Poems,* Cossy also has heard about "a big Chicago far off." One morning a stranger in town named John Embers suavely starts a conversation with her and then invites her to breakfast. An author and world-traveler, Embers sparks Cossy's imagination with his incredibly polite manners ("He sort of broke the peach. The juice didn't run down.") and with stories of his adventures abroad. After breakfast the two stroll up a hill from which he imaginatively points to New York, St. Louis, Cincinnati, New Orleans, Chicago, San Francisco, the Pacific, Japan, the Alps, London, Rome, and the Nile. Cosma Wakely's vision corroborates her name.

Returning home she finds her mother scrubbing the well-house. Repulsed, she goes next door to visit thirty-year-old Mis' Bingy, whose husband drunkenly greets her at the door with an upraised hatchet. As Cossy pushes him aside, he falls and strikes his head against the cook stove. Leaving him unconscious, Mis' Bingy grabs her infant and rushes out with Cossy. Shortly the three of them are on the train headed for Chicago.

The only job Cossy can find is printing envelopes on a Gordon press from eight until six for three dollars a week. Now she learns the kind of "emancipation" a big city offers the working girl: a dusty, foul-smelling shop, fire hazards, indecent foremen, fines, noise, and hurry hurry hurry. She joins the women in their strike for fire-escapes, sanitation, and a few cents more a week: "I tramped along with them. There was something good in the way our feet all came down on the walk together."

Unwilling to let realism sustain the novel, Zona Gale rescues Cossy by the easy trick of having the manager's wife, Mrs. Carney, pluck her from the mob and enroll her in a New York private school. Despite her wealthy new friends who show her how the upper-crust lives, Cossy still remembers the factory girls. A sudden visit from one of them who tells about a pressroom fire in which five girls burned to death, brings Cossy back from a weekend party on the Hudson in time to attend the factory meeting called to protest conditions. Cossy is considerably more educated and polished now as she stands before her former fellow workers. Her speech, however, is sheer sentimentality in its recommendations that the workers, instead of continuing their strike, seek to understand their employers as a first step toward harmony. The working girls hardly anticipated this pallid suggestion, and Zona Gale's readers easily detected her reluctance, in fiction, to replace her tired sentimentality with militant reform and realism. She goes no further in this novel than to bring Cossy and long-lost John Embers together again; both resolve after their marriage to work for "the right of the workers to growth."

Zona Gale's sensitivity to the shackles inhibiting human growth mark the direction she took in her subsequent novels. After *A Daughter of the Morning* she no longer allowed her unflagging optimism to vitiate her shock at present conditions. A new tone enters her work. In *Birth* (1918), *Miss Lulu Bett* (1920), and *Faint Perfume* (1923), her theme is human bondage as seen in the world of domestic, economic, and psychological pressures. A few years later in her fiction these shackles inhibiting freedom take on philosophic definition, so that in equating them with determinism and materialism she finds the world of spirit promising the only real freedom. While exploring the strange realms of spiritism, especially in her novel *Preface to a Life* (1926), she still remained active in state and national issues. It may be, of course, that if she had removed herself further from current hassles, she would have strengthened her art. Diving deeply can only require a plunge of one's total self. Zona Gale's spiritual explorations and, still later, her psychological wanderings down hauntingly melancholic paths leave her reader still athirst for the definitive vision.

But current issues were too compelling for Zona Gale to ignore, even though in quiet Portage she was ready to dive. Women suffrage was just such an issue. The suffrage fight got underway soon after the Civil War when the emancipation of slaves led to the question of enlarging the electorate. Led by Elizabeth Cady Stanton and Susan B. Anthony, women tried to secure petitions against the Fourteenth Amendment which, while intended to protect Negro civil rights, granted suffrage only to male citizens. Women also protested the Fifteenth Amendment which omitted the word "sex" in its guarantee that a citizen's right to vote shall not be denied because of "race, color, or previous condition of servitude." After winning their first suffrage victory in the Territory of Wyoming in 1870, women all over the nation sought to amend their own state and territorial constitutions while the National Woman Suffrage Association and the American Woman Suffrage Association kept their fire directed at Congress. The Progressive party added impetus to the movement by making women suffrage a plank in its 1912 platform. The next year in Washington Lucy Burns and Alice Paul led a parade of over five thousand women on President Wilson's inauguration day and succeeded in drawing most of the people away from the President's own parade. Finally, by exactly the two-thirds majority required, the House of Representatives passed a constitutional amendment in 1918 which, after more delay, was passed by the Senate to become in 1920 the Nineteenth Amendment to the Constitution. Women had won the vote—some 144 years after America's independence.

Though pleased, Zona Gale argued that women's battle for equal civil, legal, and political rights was only half-won. Her article published in the *Nation* two years later (Aug. 23, 1922), entitled "What Women Won in Wisconsin," pointed out that, even after the 1920 suffrage victory, a bill in the 1921 Wisconsin legislature to permit women to serve on juries was defeated. What women had won, she vehemently contrasted with what women had yet to win. She reminded readers that in Wisconsin married women were ineligible to take civil-service examinations; that they were barred from being policewomen; that a woman who had moved back into the state to receive resident-tuition rates for her son at the University was refused because her husband still lived in Montana, the law reading that where the husband lives, there too "lives" the wife; that a woman could not vote anywhere else but where her husband votes; that married women were not allowed permanent appointments to regular teaching positions.

She noted that Wisconsin was not the only state needing corrective legislation. Her roll call included Alabama: mothers are not equal guardians of children; Arkansas: inheritance laws discriminate against women; Delaware: fathers can will away children from mothers; Florida: fathers control the services and earnings of children; Louisiana: married women are classified with children and the insane as unable to contract on their own responsibility; Maryland: divorce laws discriminate against women; Massachusetts: women are ineligible for jury service; Mississippi: a husband owns his wife's services in the home and in business; Vermont: earnings of a married woman belong to her husband. Agitation of this kind plus the important suffrage victory of 1920 led to far-reaching consequences. Women's lobbies increased their effectiveness to such a degree that by the end of the decade a lobby like the Women's Joint Congressional Committee could boast of having successfully pushed through over four hundred state and local laws favoring social reform and women's rights.

In her own state of Wisconsin Miss Gale helped to write the 1923 Wisconsin Equal Rights Law intended to remove discrimination against women by granting them the same rights as men in such matters as suffrage, freedom of contract, choice of residence for voting purposes, jury service, and care and custody of children. Speaking in support of this bill before the State Bar Association, she said: "Gentlemen, in this matter there is no woman's standpoint and there is no man's standpoint. There is only the need of our common citizenship to rid our statute books of these vestiges of the old English common law and to bring our laws down to date. To do this for women—yes; and for men; and for the general welfare; and for the children and the children's children."[17] Unquestionably, Zona Gale heads the list of Wisconsin women who helped to effect this legislation.

IV

Central to all Miss Gale's non-literary interests was Wisconsin politics. Her long political activity in Wisconsin, concurrent with her literary work, started when she wrote her early Friendship Village stories. Slowly she awakened to the fact that in her own state Robert M. La Follette had been waging political warfare for over twenty years. At first she trusted the Wisconsin newspapers when they called young La Follette (he was only twenty-nine when he was first elected to the House of Representatives in 1884) a disturbing influence and a dangerous insurgent within the Republican party. Her father's insistence that they were wrong sent her searching for the facts. The job was not easy because, as she later said, "The mass of misinformation about [La Follette] equals that concerning the motions of the earth in the days of Ptolemy."[18]

Backed heavily by political bosses and corporations, the Wisconsin press opposed La Follette outright. When the powerful multimillionaire boss, Charles Pfister, bought out the state's largest independent newspaper, the Milwaukee *Sentinel,* for a huge sum in 1901, the Republican political machine headed by Philetus Sawyer, John Spooner, Henry Payne, E. W. Keyes, and Pfister removed the last obstruction in their free-wheeling effort to smear La Follette. It was not, then, through the daily newspapers that Zona Gale found the facts. Weekly copies of *La Follette's Magazine* accumulated in her parents' home. From these and from La Follette's own *Autobiography,* which had first appeared in the *American Magazine* in 1911 and then was published complete in 1912, she learned more about the indefatigable Wisconsin leader. She read the amazing story of his successful campaign waged in 1880 for the Dane County district attorney post against Boss Keynes's well-oiled machine. His record telling of his fight against the whole state Republican machine, his success in winning three consecutive terms to the House starting in 1884, and his relentless efforts to curb the power of private corporations and political bossism thrilled her.

Zona Gale read on. The incredible tale unfolded the drama behind La Follette's defeat for a fourth term in the House; his unsuccessful gubernatorial campaigns in 1894, 1896, and 1898; his victory in 1900 and, as governor, his achievement in reorganizing the state Republican party. It told of his victorious fight for railroad taxation laws which were passed in 1903 despite the unbelievably open bribery of Boss Sawyer and prominent lobbyists to sway the legislators. By providing for direct primary elections, La Follette went on the next year to demolish the machine system of politics previously giving bosses absolute power to determine in secret caucuses who would be the candidates. By the time La Follette was elected to the United States Senate in 1905, his achievements in Wisconsin became known as "the Wisconsin idea," the result of progressive Republicans and Democrats joining against the reactionary forces of both parties.

Excited by what La Follette was accomplishing, Zona Gale organized Portage women's clubs to study such issues as child labor in America, labor legislation, employers' liability, women in industry, modern prison methods, social settlements—in a word, as she wrote in *La Follette's Magazine* (Aug. 7, 1909), to study "living, breathing, human America." Soon she was characterizing La Follette's program as "politics socialized" which, she maintained, regarded human life and its right to grow as more important than property rights. She interpreted the history of La Follette's career as a fight against special privilege seeking advantage for the few at the expense of the many. In Progressivism she found that an ethical principle had been made into a political faith. She recognized Wisconsin as a state-wide laboratory, an experiment station for this faith.

La Follette's voice in Wisconsin was the voice of the West, termed by Woodrow Wilson in 1911 as "the voice of protest."[19] Popularly it was known as the spirit that raised more hell than corn. It vitalized the early Granger Movements, the Farmers' Alliances, the Greenbacks, and the Populists, and it set many a farmer to reading Edward Bellamy's *Looking Backward* (1888), Henry George's *Progress and Poverty* (1879), and Ignatius Donnelly's *Caesar's Column* (1891). It reached an unforgettable climax at the Populist Convention on July 9, 1896, when its presidential candidate, William Jennings Bryan, closed his speech with the spellbinding image: "You shall not press down upon the brow of labor this cross of thorns, you shall not crucify mankind upon a cross of gold!"

The voice of Bryan and the West demanded an answer to the question, "What is democracy?" No answer would satisfy unless it came to terms with legislative reforms (1) removing special business interest groups from government, (2) making government more responsible to the people, (3) broadening economic and social welfare.[20] Bryan's voice was not silenced by William McKinley's victory at the polls; an impressive number of Middle West intellectuals seeking the same reforms added to it. At the University of Wisconsin, Richard T. Ely, who had been attacked as a "radical" at Johns Hopkins, became the director of the School of Economics, Political Science, and History; and as a liberal he pioneered work in taxation, conservation, municipal ownership, tariffs, and labor relations. John R. Commons, Ely's assistant at Johns Hopkins, joined him at the University of Wisconsin to give direction to progressive politics. From the Middle West came historian J. Allen Smith, an outspoken Populist, and Vernon Lewis Parrington whose *Main Currents in American Thought*, written later in far-away Seattle, interpreted American civilization from a strongly agrarian viewpoint. Thorstein Veblen, John Dewey, Clarence Darrow, Henry Lloyd, Washington Gladden, Jane Addams, Walter Rauschenbusch—each in his own way—supported the principles of Progressivism. And each, at one time or another, bore the label of "radical" and was summarily vilified.

Busier than even the University of Chicago as a center for liberal politics was the Madison campus where President John Bascom's influence inspired his successors, Thomas Chamberlain, Charles Kendall Adams, and Charles R. Van Hise, all dedicated to "the Wisconsin idea." Throughout La Follette's political life he chose consultants from the University. As governor he formed a "lunch club" of professors and legislators which met weekly to study political issues affecting the state. In 1912 thirty-seven university professors held posts in the state government. In this close association with intellectuals La Follette was like other Progressive leaders in the region: Albert Cummins of Iowa, Albert Beveridge of Indiana, George Norris of Nebraska. They were sharp, well-educated men adept in legislative subtleties and supported by astute advisors. This was generally not the case among earlier Populists and Grangers.[21]

Zona Gale, herself a University of Wisconsin graduate familiar with Bascom's liberal influence, slowly moved into the La Follette camp. It was too soon in 1908 for her to become involved in the Taft–La Follette schism in the Republican party. Nor was she swept into the 1912 campaign which saw Theodore Roosevelt's last-minute duplicity undermine La Follette's chances to be nominated as the Progressive's candidate for presidential election. Most important was her growing interest in La Follette's minority platform, which was thrown out as too "socialistic" by Taft Republicans during the 1908 national convention. She agreed with La Follette that corruption and favoritism should be eliminated from national politics, and she favored welfare reforms, tariff revision, and revaluation of railroad property for taxation—plans for which La Follette was bitterly fighting, against such dedicated opposition as the National Association of Manufacturers, the National Metal Trades, the Citizens Alliance, the Citizens Industrial Association, and a host of other powerful groups backed by wealthy conservatives.

More than anything else La Follette did, his lonely "No" vote on April 5, 1916, highlighted Zona Gale's admiration for him. Only La Follette and five other senators voted that day against declaring war on Germany. For this action the Wisconsin senator was of course called a pacifist. When the Associated Press misquoted his extemporaneous speech given on September 20, 1917, in St. Paul, Minnesota, he loomed as a downright disloyal American. In a thousand newspapers across the country headlines quoted La Follette as having said that America had "no" grievances against Germany, when, in fact, he had shouted, "I don't mean to say that we hadn't suffered grievances; we had—at the hands of Germany. Serious grievances!"[22] Miss Gale, herself a pacifist, was shocked by the lamentable aftermath.

Immediately La Follette was attacked from all sides. Newspapers screamed his disloyalty. The hometown Madison *Democrat* and *Wisconsin State Journal* printed libelous smears. Parades in Madison held aloft such slogans as: "La Follette misrepresents Wisconsin! GET HIM OUT!" and "La Follette is one of only a few SLACKERS IN WISCONSIN!"[23] From around the country such groups as chambers of commerce, Rotary and Kiwanis, Councils of Defense, Grand Army veterans, merchants' and manufacturers' associations united to demand his expulsion from the U. S. Senate. Thousands of petitions flooded the Senate's Committee on Privileges and Elections, demanding not censure but impeachment. Senators Frank Kellogg of Minnesota and Joseph Robinson of Arkansas made unrestrained tirades from the Senate floor. Kellogg and others traveled around the country denouncing La Follette. Senators Henry Cabot Lodge and John Weeks worked strenuously to remove La Follette; their Massachusetts State Republican Convention in October passed unanimously a resolution condemning the Wisconsin senator "as of comfort to the common enemy, the imperial German government, and as of marked disloyalty to his country, the United States of America."[24] In the background was Theodore Roosevelt, enjoying immensely all this tempest against his former political competitor.

A crueler cut came from the University of Wisconsin where many of La Follette's intimate friends, including former President Charles R. Van Hise, signed a statement accusing him of disloyalty. Most astonishing was the action of the Vigilantes, a group of prominent authors who organized in November, 1916, to fight with their pens "for their country's honor and their country's life."[25] The founders were Herman Hagedorn, Porter Emerson Browne, Charles Hanson Towne, and Julian Street; but this number was soon enlarged to include Samuel Hopkins Adams, Mary Austin, Gertrude Atherton, Hamlin Garland, George Ade, Rex Beach, Irvin S. Cobb, and Booth Tarkington. Zona Gale's name was significantly absent. With Theodore Roosevelt's generous contribution of funds, their first project had been to write newspaper articles favoring universal military training. But when the La Follette issue exploded, they trained their pens on him. The Washington *Post*, New York *Times*, and New York *Tribune* were among the newspapers which printed letters written by the Vigilantes denouncing La Follette in such terms as a "magnificent" seditionist, a victim of "distorted mental machinery." To be expected, their virulent pens were also called up by such organizations as the United States Chamber of Commerce, the American Bankers Association, and the American Defense Society.

Truth is the sweetest revenge. The next spring after his fateful St. Paul address, Senator La Follette finally proved with stenographic records, made at the time, that he had been misquoted.

Without fanfare the Associated Press quickly apologized for its "regrettable" error. Similar apologies poured in. Final vindication came in 1922 when Wisconsin sent him back to the Senate for a fourth term; he carried every county in the state and polled the largest majority of votes ever given a Wisconsin candidate.

Zona Gale worked hard for his re-election in 1922. She traveled throughout the state giving speeches in his behalf. An even greater effort on her part came in 1924 when La Follette headed the Progressive ticket for the presidency.

That year at the Republican Convention Calvin Coolidge's nomination was a cut-and-dried affair. While the Democratic delegates were deadlocked in choosing their presidential candidate, La Follette declared his candidacy as an Independent. He had been reluctant to make this public declaration until he knew whether or not the Democrats would nominate a Progressive. While the Democrats were still deadlocked early in July, Zona Gale and other members of the La Follette for President Committee brought to his home in Washington a box containing petitions bearing over two hundred thousand signatures of persons wanting him to declare his candidacy. In her account of this visit for the *Nation,* she quoted the Committee's chairman, W. T. Rawleigh, as saying to La Follette: "On behalf of more than two hundred thousand American citizens . . . we turn to you . . . the one man big enough and strong enough and courageous enough to drive the money changers out of the temple of the government and restore it cleansed to the service of the people."[26]

The strongest organization encouraging La Follette to throw his hat into the ring was the Conference for Progressive Political Action led by Norman Hapgood, Felix Frankfurter, Jane Addams, Oswald Garrison Villard, and Louis Brandeis. To the C.P.P.A.'s Cleveland convention came La Follette's son, Robert Jr., who read his father's platform to the cheering nine thousand visitors and delegates. The next day, July 5, the convention endorsed Senator La Follette's candidacy by acclamation. Immediately pledges of support flooded his office. Mrs. Mabel Costigan, for example, informed him that she had organized more than seventy women to work on his campaign, her executive committee including Zona Gale, Jane Addams, Mary Drier, and Florence Kelley.

With her 1921 Pulitzer Prize establishing her literary prominence, Zona Gale found herself in demand as a lecturer. Soft-spoken but wonderously articulate, she addressed groups in Wisconsin and neighboring states. Audiences listened to her with affection as she, in turn, recited La Follette's record. Her repeated theme stressed the urgency for his political program to check rampant conservatism which had brought victory to business after the war. She pointed out that most of La Follette's reform measures, for which he had been called "radical" and "Red," were now law. She predicted that again in this campaign his platform calling for public ownership of the nation's water power and other national resources, for recovery of the Navy's oil reserves and other parts of the public domain fraudulently transferred to private interests, for house-cleaning in the departments of Justice and the Interior, for public ownership of railroads, and for rights of farmers and industrial workers to bargain collectively would again be received by conservatives with jeers and catcalls.

To reinforce her efforts she published a spate of articles during the campaign. "Correspondence Drafting La Follette" appeared in a July issue of the *Nation*. "Conservatives' Paradise" in the following month's issue of the *World Tomorrow* cited the La Follette-Wheeler (Burton K.) ticket as the only channel open for liberals. She acidly recalled a previous time, in 1912, when a similar channel opened, but then Bull Moose Roosevelt "betrayed" them in his kinship with Henry Cabot Lodge. In October the *New Republic* published "Why I Shall Vote For La Follette," and in November "La Follette's Vindication" was printed in *Forum*.

"Fighting Bob" La Follette's five million votes were less than those cast for John W. Davis, the Democratic candidate, and were only a third the number given Coolidge. The next year La Follette was dead. But widely known was Zona Gale's profound respect for his achievements and for his kind of political philosophy translated into "the Wisconsin idea" and national Progressivism.

CHAPTER 4

On to Realism

I

"WHERE, oh where, is 'Friendship Village'?" asked the New York *Sun* (April 6, 1919) when Zona Gale's *Birth* appeared in 1918. "It is where it ought to be, along with Pelleas and Etarre, 'way back in the past,' " was the *Sun's* own answer. "Thank heavens she killed them off [the Friendship Villagers] long ago, and got down to brass tacks in *Birth*," observed the *Bookman* reviewer.[1] "After an evening spent with the Friendship Village folks one felt like bolting to the nearest delicatessen shop for a dill pickle," wrote a Springfield (Mass.) *Union* reviewer (Dec. 29, 1918), who then continued: "In *Birth*, Miss Gale has herself supplied the pickle, and given us a section of small-town life in which the sweet and the bitter are wholesomely and realistically blended."

This novel marks an important turning point in Miss Gale's fiction. No longer is there the syrup which smothered so many of her Friendship Village stories. *Birth* led her away from the primrose path that brought fabulous success to several of her contemporary women novelists. Novels like Kate Douglas Wiggin's *Rebecca of Sunnybrook Farm* (1903), Gene Stratton-Porter's *Girl of the Limberlost* (1909) and *Michael O'Halloran* (1915), and Kathleen Norris' *Pollyanna* (1913)—each numbering over a million sales—were as sentimental and expansively optimistic as Zona Gale's early work. But too much was happening for her to sustain this tone herself. War, social and economic muckraking, and bitter political battles had created a new atmosphere inconsistent with idealized small-town togetherness. As a turning point *Birth* opened a period of serious literary realism for Zona Gale—the same year that Zane Grey's *U.P. Trail* was breaking sales records.

Her small town now is named Burage, "etched mercilessly but

fairly" wrote Professor Arthur Quinn.[2] Unless transformed by an alchemic dawn or a rich moon, unobserved by most, it is a dull place of trival routine. Women water their plants. Ministers make their expected calls, faithfully recording them in their little books. A horse-drawn dray creaks and bumps under the elms. Burage is laid bare, its only center of mystery being its railway station where trains leave for far-off Chicago. But lying under a burning afternoon sun, its waiting room squalid and its freight cars baking on the track, the station is more often the center of ugliness and desolation.

No longer a picturesque little village sleeping by the Wisconsin River, Burage resembles in its grimness the border towns of E. W. Howe and Edwin Arlington Robinson. In writing *Birth*, Zona Gale joined these realists in their protest against what William Allen White called "the smugness of the pastoral writers who told of the delights of the rural scene."[3] In Burage the social and emotional delights have stagnated into meaningless rituals, gossip, and teas. "Business is business" describes the predatory level of its morality. Someone energetic and idealistic enough to seek beauty, especially by creating it himself, encounters only the condescending smiles of culturally arid busybodies. It is a place Sinclair Lewis' Carol Kennicott would recognize; its stern provinciality is a trap.

The dominant characteristic of its citizens is littleness, but on two levels. There is, of course, the littleness seen in Mis' Monument Miles, Mis' True, Mis' Barber, Mis' Copper—with their small talk and pettiness. Though they naturally see themselves as the "big" ladies of Burage, they are blessedly imperceptive to the utter inconsequence of their coffee-spoon lives. Nothing but little people on Main Street, their masks are ripped off to reveal their puny aspirations. But another kind of littleness, essential to this novel's design, is the littleness of human will, strength, knowledge, power. Willy-nilly, people are buffeted, teased, wrecked, impelled. Against the gods they stand naked and terribly vulnerable. Fate determines their lives. Accidental circumstances irrevocably lead to consequences unknown and uncontrollable by the helpless victim.

In *Birth* this victim of deterministic forces is Marshall Pitt. He comes to Burage a stranger, a door-to-door salesman, his sample case weighted with pickle and fruit products. Somewhere, five hundred miles away or more, he has a father with whom he had never "got on," a step-mother "such as she was," and a younger brother he only likes well enough to bully. On a sticky afternoon he fatefully knocks on the door of Miss Rachel Arrowsmith, a woman of breeding. Instead of sending him on his way, she invites him in for a cool glass of tea. Wet and faint from the intolerable heat, this little man with colossal but indeterminate longings who has been tossed to this threshold, now mechanically crosses it. Sitting inside with Miss Arrowsmith is Barbara Ellsworth whose father's recent death has smitten her with agonizing loneliness. Pitt immediately recognizes in her and himself "two little beings" alone in an indifferent world. Dimly aware of something within him—something Zona Gale would describe as a fundamental power embryonic only because it is not used—he dreams that by marrying Barbara the two can stand together against the willy-nilly world.

"Subject to wild, random forces," like Carrie Meeber in Theodore Dreiser's *Sister Carrie*, Pitt's new wife centers her overruling passions upon fine clothes, bright lights, and glamor. She is unconscious of Pitt's tormenting struggle to find significance within himself. In her opinion his crude inarticulateness —"aphasia," critic Régis Michaud calls it—[4] proves his littleness. Certain only that he will never be able to give her her heart's desires, she deserts him for a smooth-talking itinerant bandmaster. Abandoned with his year-old son Jeffrey, Pitt is utterly incapable of understanding what has happened: "the little man's ineffectualness was tragic." He had no "armor." Guilt-ridden, his only explanation was that in some way he was responsible.

The novel's second section treats Jeffrey's upbringing in Mis' Copper's household while Pitt prospects for gold in Alaska. The child's rampant imagination entertains visions of himself as Sir Galahad, a cup above his bed as the Holy Grail. But in time Burage's aridity blights the young boy, who rationalizes that his early passions of activity amounted to nothing and that, in fact, he is useless. His imagination paralyzed, his interest in school and in "sketching" depleted, he goes to work in a miserable Burage dry cleaning and dyeing business operated by wretchedly dishonest Mr. Beck. His future holds only the hope that someday his unknown father will return from "a white, unvisualized North."

In the third section Pitt and Jeffrey are united, but only momentarily. A chasm opens between father and son, for Pitt is puzzled about his own failure to elicit warmth from his son, and Jeffrey is disillusioned about his father. Pitt's commonplace manner, his inarticulateness, his plodding heaviness fail to match Jeffrey's expectations concerning a father home from distant gold fields. Applying the standards of Jeffrey's world as he knows it, he can only conclude that "this was not the way a fellow's father ought to be." By comparison, Bennie Bierce's father was "a hustling, red-cheeked, ready-to-wear garment representative."

Much like a Greek play, tragic ironies reminiscent also of Thomas Hardy's baleful fiction mysteriously weave their sombre effects. Early in the novel, for example, Pitt looks at the abandoned baby Jeffrey and helplessly cries, "born of a chance pity in Rachel Arrowsmith for a wretched little salesman of pickle and fruit products." Or again, after he has returned empty-handed to Burage, he tells about his once having switched land claims with his partner in Alaska. From his new claim he received nothing, while after the exchange his partner struck it rich. "I guess he won't come much short of a couple of hundred thousand—mebbe more. . . . Seems queer, don't it?" When he suddenly receives word that Barbara has been lying ill for six weeks in a Chicago hospital, he rushes to her but arrives too late. Musing on the fact that for years he had known nothing of Barbara's whereabouts, he faces the stars and wonders why he missed her dying words by only five hours. His desperate wish for proof that she thought the family trio still inviolate would remain unfulfilled.

Pitt burned to death for a dog. ("Well, but of all the fool things. For a *dog*. . . .") Miss Arrowsmith, as if leading an agonized chorus, explained to dazed Jeffrey that if she had not gone for some gentians, Jep the dog would not have been caught in her burning house and Pitt would still be alive. As counterpoint, Jeffrey fingers in his pocket a little package he had neglected to give his father earlier that same tragic day. Sent from the Chicago hospital where Barbara had died, it contained the necklace of pearls Pitt had given to her as a wedding present. Upon the pearls lay a note which Jeffrey read: "Marshall and Jeffrey—love—Mother."

The crucial irony comes with Pitt's dying words, "Am I going to die—like a fool?" (The novel's closing line is Mis' Monument Miles's judgment, "Pitt never was much good.") That behind his foolishness lay a great soul which had vainly struggled for freedom shocks Jeffrey, who had been embarrassed, even repulsed, by his father's common clay. No one but Rachel Arrowsmith, the middle-aged spinster, had perceived Pitt's essential quality. Now, in death, Pitt's spirit sears Jeffrey's flesh, awakening in him the true knowledge of his father's bigness. Now Jeffrey understands why his father had never lost faith that Barbara, regardless of her desertion, was yet an angel. Coming to Jeffrey now is the knowledge of tragedy, defined not as the failure of the aspiring soul but rather of a "soul, which, having power, will not venture." This same knowledge, this sense, which cuts through all inequalities of intellect, Pitt possessed. Now held by Jeffrey, it serves to free him.

Zona Gale's publisher (Macmillan) urged her to alter the novel's title, predicting that its meaninglessness would kill a fine work. Despite the warning that the novel, bearing the title "Birth," "sounds like a treatise by Mrs. Sanger" and that "in many a small town library it is catalogued under Eugenics,"[5] she remained adamant. She would not budge, even to the suggestion for "Mr. Marshall Pitt." "In my book called *Birth*," she wrote, "the whole novel hinges on the 'birth'—the second birth—of the boy Jeffrey."[6] This moment comes when Jeffrey, starting out for Chicago with his newly won discovery about his father, feels that "the dawn's great moment had arrived."

> The heavens were so open that from distant north to distant south there rolled dawn upon dawn, and deep in the east came manifold dawns to flame and pass. His the only watching eye in those great fields of sky and stubble, Jeffrey had a sense of overflowing all boundaries, and of himself joining in the surge and color of the hour. The lawless motion of the train half-freed him from space. He felt some power never known to him.

Even in later years Zona Gale considered *Birth* her best novel. Unquestionably it is her pivotal work. Her readers finally learned she could write a realistic novel, and it was this happy evidence which leavened their enthusiasm. Noting her new disposition to deal justly with character and action, they wondered if she could sustain this authenticity. They anticipated an even more "realistic" novel and were sure, when *Miss Lulu Bett* appeared two years later, that now at last Zona Gale had proved herself a writer whose stature demanded their serious appraisal. What they did not know was that the realism in *Miss Lulu Bett,* stinging and devastating as it was, hid a strain of mysticism which was to surface again in *Preface to a Life.*

In their enthusiasm for *Birth* and its promise of even more unromantic things to come, the readers paid little attention to the essential point of *Birth.* Undergirding this novel, even with all its pictures of small-town unpleasantness, is her belief in a world of spirit infusing and thereby unifying all things. Awakening to this discovery is to be born again; it is to sing Whitman's "Song of Myself," certain that one's essential spirit is fused with an absolute Spirit. What then of a universe in which, as Rachel Arrowsmith asks Jeffrey, "your father's death, his marriage, your existence [was] dependent on a whim of mine"? One's "whim," a word Emerson recommended be carved on every lintel, is safely guided by nature's laws whose "dice are always loaded." Therefore, despite the apparent accidents of fortune, Jeffrey echoes the Emersonian certainty that behind Miss Arrowsmith's whims "the guiding impulse was there."

Birth was the kind of book Miss Gale had been waiting to write, one which would balance the mundane and the mystical. Her temperament leaned toward the latter; reviewers hailed the former. Her decision to follow the reviewers' lead—to write a story stripped of all romance, to employ a prose style as monotonously stark as the lives of the characters she would depict—resulted in the overwhelming irony of Zona Gale's career. The book archly responsible for her literary reputation was a *tour de force,* intended to play the balance as far toward the mundane as she could go. Her success was public. Privately she knew she would sometime write another *Birth.*

II

Early in 1919 Zona Gale began sending her new manuscript on its rounds to magazine editors, her cover-letter typically restrained: "Dear Sir:—I am submitting with this a novelette, 'Miss Lulu Bett,' with the hope that it may just possibly be acceptable to you."[7] Six editors rejected it straightaway, even though it could have been run as a magazine serial. Finally Rutger Jewett of D. Appleton Company agreed to publish it as a book.

For the story Zona Gale had taken an episode originally intended for *Birth* but cut out to shorten the already too lengthy novel. Jeffrey Pitt became Bobby in *Miss Lulu Bett*; and the title character was his casual aunt in *Birth* changed to the leading character in the novelette. Carefully she expanded the episode, which in its completion was still "as spare," thought Carl Van Doren, "as the virgin frame" of the heroine.[8] Wilson Follett and other friends had warned her that another long novel would probably have the same unprofitable fate as *Birth*. This advice, which augmented her previous resolution to strip away the fanciful, left her with forty-five thousand lean words, the length of Edith Wharton's *Ethan Frome* and Willa Cather's *A Lost Lady*, with which Zona Gale's story was later favorably compared.

Because of meager sales with her preceding novels, booksellers were skeptical about this one. But with the vigorous promotion which her new publisher gave it, plus the burst of favorable reviews, it soon competed as a best seller with Lewis' *Main Street*, published also in 1920. Without hesitation reviewers thought it the best novel Zona Gale had yet done; furthermore, it promised them that she had forever cast sentimentality behind her, that she was unquestionably finished with Friendship Village. They read the new novel as a tart picture of small-town American life, and as first-rate realism. Nothing now interfered with her straightforward expression—no sentimentality, no distracting threads of mysticism, no contrived optimism, no tiresome chatter, and no tea parties. In it instead were realism's sordidness and triviality, its tragedy of unfulfilled lives, its hypocrisies, its mundane and dish-water monotony. Writing five months after the novel appeared, Robert Benchley in the New York *World* (July 10, 1920) apologized for merely hailing it as "a great book." "But I can't do anything else. I'm very sorry." His wry point was that for five solid months the same adjective had been used. Constance Rourke a month later summarized the attitude generated about the book by stating flatly, "Whatever its antecedents, the book stands as a signal accomplishment in American letters."[9]

A "portent" to Miss Rourke of even firmer work to come, *Miss Lulu Bett* also reinforced the current hue and cry over women's rights. Her most successful treatment of woman's plight comes in this novel. No longer does Friendship Village, with its kindness and goodwill, befriend the newly educated American woman —nor do its comforting niceties satisfy her. The "home town" now tyrannizes her. What was once familial harmony is now in *Miss Lulu Bett* snapping and peevish incivility. Worse still, the chances for escape are few, the hopes gigantically disproportionate to their realization.

After fifteen years in her sister's and brother-in-law's household, Lulu Bett, unmarried at thirty-three, presents a sad spectacle of the frustrated, unemancipated woman. When old Mr. Bett died, Lulu and her senile mother moved in with Ina and Dwight Deacon who routinely assumed that, for her "keep," Lulu would take over all the menial domestic chores. Her stirrings of rebellion offer no hope, for the pattern of small-town mores dictates her duty to the household. She is its only competent person, its workhorse, but no one pays attention. She has long ago sacrificed her pride to Dwight's grossness. Virtually a slave having no means of liberation, she stoically submits to the treadmill. Her own summary, "Nobody cares what becomes of me after they're fed," echoes the old woman in Sherwood Anderson's story, "Death in the Woods." Demeaned and scorned, the butt of jokes, both women represent figures found in a social captivity which deprives them of individuality and relevance.

It is not surprising that when Dwight's brother, Ninian, comes to visit the family, Lulu's expectations stir. Ninian has traveled for twenty years, has been to all the places John Embers described to provincial Cosma Wakely in *A Daughter of the Morning*, and has now returned with endless stories to tell. Though lacking the capacity for intensive observation, he has nevertheless been away, to alien lands. Incredulous that Lulu has never left Warbleton, merely another Portage-Katytown-Burage, he lightly suggests a trip to the city with Dwight and Ina. Symbolizing liberation, the big city dazzles Lulu; with her companions, she sees *Peter Pan*, chosen by Ninian because the tickets were expensive. Later the four go to a restaurant where, as a gag, Dwight performs a marriage ceremony for Lulu and Ninian. Startled to discover its legality, since Dwight *is* a justice of the peace, flushed and tremulous Lulu accedes to Ninian's wish to consider themselves married. Ironically for helpless Lulu, that which was intended as a joke becomes a marriage; brassy ragtime music is her wedding march.

A month later when Lulu returns to Warbleton without her husband, the Deacons are shocked to learn from her that Ninian was already married and has gone to Oregon to learn if his wife is still alive. Caring nothing for Lulu's torment, Dwight thinks only of the gossip Lulu's return will set afoot. "I desire that you should keep silent and protect my family from scandal," he thunders. But the neighbors' curiosity cannot be curbed.

"Lulu Bett!" Or, "W-well, it *isn't* Lulu Bett any more, is it? Well, what are you doing here? I thought. . . ."

"I'm back to stay," she said.

"The idea! Well, where are you hiding that handsome husband of yours? Say, but we were surprised! You're the sly one—"

"My—Mr. Deacon isn't here."

"Oh."

"No. He's West."

"Oh, I see."

While waiting to hear from Ninian, Lulu meets Neil Cornish, the new music store proprietor whom the Deacons regard as an eligible husband for Di, Dwight's eighteen-year-old daughter by an earlier marriage. Cornish, however, attends to Lulu when, for example, after dining with the Deacons he joins her at the piano in singing such tender classics as "Long, Long Ago" and "Little Nell of Narragansett Bay." More importantly, he recognizes the stifling Deacon household and Lulu's intolerable role in it as a parody of the old-fashioned "historical home," a haven transformed into a trap. She discovers in Cornish a sensitivity and intelligence rare indeed in prosaic Warbleton. She tells him about her bizarre marriage to Ninian and her present anxiousness to hear from him. When Ninian finally writes to Lulu that their marriage is absolved because he has found his wife who had deserted him, she and Cornish marry. Lulu leaves the household welter to her inept sister and serenely gives to her shattered brother-in-law the task of rebuilding his respectability among his gossiping neighbors who will be agog at learning of his brother's bigamy.

Zona Gale's characterizations are economical and strong. Lulu is what Fannie Hurst called the "shining star" reflected in greasy reality."[10] She mitigates the family's heavily weighted banality with an ingenuousness which Henry James enjoyed portraying in his young, unmarried women. By contrast, the boorishness of Dwight Deacon, the village's prototypal business-man, prevents his ever transcending the maudlin or the tire-somely respectable. Ina is weak and simpering, able to do little but feed Dwight's own image of self-importance. Old Mrs. Bett, shriveled and disaffectionate, occasionally "sasses" Dwight but is herself a narrow-minded person given to "tantrims." The daughter Di apes sophistication in an unsuccessful elopement with Bobby Larkin, the neighbor boy, but her intentions only reveal a sauci-ness nurtured by her father. Little Monona, daughter of Ina and Dwight, is a whiny, recalcitrant pest. In short, the traditional family hearth as the center of peace is now a stage upon which dull-witted, thoroughly bourgeois fools do their strutting.

Zona Gale's angular and staccato style, her stark brevity, art-fully project these characterizations. Embroidery is cut away, and what remains is "a hard little picture," a term Edith Wharton used when writing to Miss Gale about the novel.[11] But Miss Wharton was uneasy about it too, even though she praised her for the sharpness of the picture's edges. She cautioned her that at this "turning-point" she must avoid stripping her style to the point of barrenness. In her opinion this was what Zona Gale had done in *Miss Lulu Bett*. "I resent this," Miss Wharton continued, in her own Jamesian way, "first because you have needlessly limited your field of expression, and produced an impression of monotony in your style as well as in the lives of the people you depict; and secondly, because it is to this telegraphic brevity, and to this poverty of vocabulary, that hurry, laziness and ignorance of the history of our language and its boundless re-sources, are inevitably leading all our young writers. . . ."

Miss Wharton, who had won the Pulitzer Prize in 1920 for her novel *The Age of Innocence*, was inveighing against the notion that a denuded subject needs a denuded style. She was far too acute to suggest that Zona Gale's earlier filigree enhanced char-acterization: she readily acknowledged *Miss Lulu Bett* as a major literary achievement, a "turning-point." Her warning was directed toward a style lacking "inflections, modulations, twists, turns, surprises, heights and depths." Even a mediocre mind such as Dwight Deacon's, she would insist, is the result of invisible accumulations and its atmosphere the totality of innumerable experiences. She wanted Zona Gale to subtilize the picture, not simply to etch it. The Jamesian "figure in the carpet," elusive as it is, would never show if the carpet itself lacked texture. And Miss Wharton was at a loss to find texture in a passage like this, from *Miss Lulu Bett*:

> "Baked potatoes," said Mr. Deacon. "That's good—that's good. The baked potato contains more nourishment than potatoes prepared in any other way. The nourishment is next to the skin. Roasting retains it."
> "That's what I always think," said his wife pleasantly.
> For fifteen years they had agreed about this.

It is important to know that Edith Wharton wrote this letter in September, 1922, more than two years after *Miss Lulu Bett* first appeared. By this time, Zona Gale had successfully adapted it for the stage; she had written another lean novelette entitled *Man at Red Barns* which *The Delineator* had run serially; and she had also sent off the manuscript of *Faint Perfume* to Glenn Frank, editor of *Century Magazine*. In other words, for nearly three years she had been experimenting with her new style, fully appreciating that it had implemented her literary success.

Yet Miss Wharton's words disturbed her. In her reply she said she was, in fact, under the "spell" of the letter.[12] Two weeks later she confessed to Miss Wharton that her criticism of *Miss Lulu Bett* had come "at precisely the moment I needed it, was restless because of the need of it." Then, pointedly, she added, "Since my new book [*Faint Perfume*] left my hand I have been haunted by just this verbal insufficiency, unwise compression, inflexibility, monotony."[13] The style bringing her literary fame dissatisfied her. For Robert Benchley to praise her for having dared to create a Dwight Deacon who says "the gorgeously conventional thing with epoch-making dullness"[14] only increased her own uncertainty, now provoked by Edith Wharton.

Regardless of these misgivings, Zona Gale believed her novel to be an honest portrayal of the duty-bound, domestically enslaved woman of her day. Its impact satisfied her. When New

York producer, Brock Pemberton, wired her on October 27, 1920, that she should adapt it for the theater, she immediately set to work. "I'm almost ashamed," she told Keene Sumner, "to say how quickly it was done. I finished it in a week, but as I wasn't satisfied with the last act I held it over from Saturday to Monday to revise it. So I can say that it took me ten days, and that doesn't sound quite so bad."[15] Another wire from Pemberton on November 13 said he would look for actors and a theater at once. On December 27 the play opened at the Belmont Theater in New York. Five months later she won the Pulitzer Prize for it.

She had had practically no writing experience for the stage. Six years earlier she had written the one-act drama called *The Neighbors,* which had been produced by the Wisconsin Dramatic Society and taken on tour through several states. Yet so adroitly did she shape this first full-length theatrical effort that it ran for some six hundred performances in New York and on the road, and it brought her royalties amounting to nearly six thousand dollars.

For the dramatic adaptation Zona Gale retained the same terse expression to depict the banality of the Deacons. Minor changes bring Neil Cornish into the play sooner, arrange Lulu's marriage to Ninian in the Deacon kitchen instead of in a big-city restaurant, and soften the character of old Mrs. Bett. Missing is the novel's romantic ending with Lulu as the new Mrs. Cornish. Instead, Lulu first receives word that Ninian has found his wife, then she leaves the Deacon family and, bewilderingly liberated, goes alone into the world to find work. As the curtain falls, old Mrs. Bett turns to helpless Ina and snickers, "Who's going to do your work now, I'd like to know?"

Miss Gale did not intend the paradoxical ending in *Miss Lulu Bett,* the novel, to suggest that Lulu's liberation from one household only sends her into the confinement of another. She thought that Lulu's marriage to Cornish constituted a "happy ending"—something hardly credible after she had depicted what domestic oppression is really like. In the play, however, the unromantic ending creates a more artful ambiguity. Is Lulu free? With no job and no husband, what are her chances? Will love and marriage, or a job paying wages, sustain her freedom? Or must she inevitably again be trapped? Ludwig Lewisohn correctly pointed out that this is "a weightier and more severe ending" than the novel's.[16]

But rumors convinced Zona Gale after the second week that the public thought this ending too depressing. So she rewrote it! In the new third act Ninian discovers that because his unnecessary first spouse has obligingly been dead for many years, he can return to rescue Lulu from her drudgery. Lulu achieves respectable wifehood, this time as Mrs. Ninian Deacon.

Immediately a torrent of criticism broke. Heywood Broun in the New York *Tribune* (Feb. 6, 1921) thought that employing the "happy ending" tradition was about as sensible as demanding feathers on a mountain lion. Lewisohn argued that Miss Gale's new twist destroyed Lulu's significant liberation.[17] Alexander Woolcott in the New York *Times* (Dec. 28, 1920) called the whole play "sleazily put together," an opinion which the rewritten last act failed to change. In a parody on Zona Gale's confusion over her heroine's destiny, Louis Untermeyer has Lulu say: " 'We'—she flushed suddenly—'my first husband and I—I think it was my first husband, although the play and the book and the lady wrote about me mixed me up sort of about myself.' "[18] The occasion brought other criticism: that Lulu's fifteen years with the Deacons proved her own lack of initiative, and that the story was only propaganda for the feminist movement.

To her scoffers Miss Gale gave straightforward answers. In no way apologizing for her revised act, she publicly replied in the New York *Tribune* (Jan. 21, 1921) that "the common experience affords as many examples of marriage as of going out into the world alone." Irony, satire, tragedy "must constitute many and many a curtain. But not all." To the charge that Lulu's treadmill cannot represent women's plight because it presupposes a witless Lulu, she sharply replied: "Do you mind my saying: 'I know them' . . . overshadowed, browbeaten women, wives or Lulus" enslaved by duty, "dead duty." And to the charge of propaganda, she averred that the story merely shows one woman, Lulu, anxious about herself.

As is to be expected, the storm increased the play's popularity. Months of solid booking made it a contender for the Pulitzer Prize. Among several other productions creating lively response the same season were *Emperor Jones* by Eugene O'Neill, who had won the Pulitzer Prize the previous year for *Beyond the Horizon*; Frank Craven's *The First Year*; and Porter Emerson Browne's *The Bad Men*. But it was *Miss Lulu Bett* that attracted the most favor with Hamlin Garland, Robert Morss Lovett, and Stuart Sherman—the group appointed to recommend the best play of 1921 to the Pulitzer Prize Committee. Though the decision to recommend Miss Gale's work was unanimous, Garland expressed disappointment with the way she "had fumbled about for a 'happy ending.' "[19]

Again the New York critics stormed. Heywood Broun in the *Tribune* (June 1, 1921) led the pack by declaring that only a few would agree with the committee's choice. To dull his attack upon Miss Gale but to sharpen it upon the committee, he argued that *Miss Lulu Bett,* the novel, might better have been the committee's choice for fiction the preceding year instead of Miss Wharton's *The Age of Innocence*. This cross-fire grew too hot for Zona Gale, who had been in New York most of the time since the play's opening five months earlier. With the prize money of $1,000 she was only too ready to hurry back to her Portage home adjacent to the silently flowing Wisconsin River.

Zona Gale's public image now appeared to be clearly set; Wisconsin had no other woman to match it. A La Follette supporter, a Progressive, a pacifist, a leader in women's rights and suffrage, the author of more than a dozen books, a Pulitzer Prize-winning dramatist—these were the unmistakable hallmarks of this slightly built, modest Portage woman. New to the image was Zona Gale as the iconoclast, one who was cutting into bourgeois Babbittry to find it both mean and vulgar. While formerly a small-town romanticist, she had now boldly come forth as a skeptic of American values in the 1920's. She saw in the times—as did H. L. Mencken and Lewis—a flabby degeneration of nineteenth-century idealism. Her futile attempt to reconcile America's traditional faith in human dignity with the newer instances of exploitation and Darwinian competitiveness aroused her disgust toward the reincarnated American hero, the man of business, who, typically, like Cyrus Harkness in her *Man at Red Barns* pontificated, "I hope to thunder the time'll come when we can have a real business man in every pulpit." Her fiction during this period showed that, in America, vices had become virtues: deceit in business was hailed as shrewdness;

generosity was belittled as evidence of unmanliness. Her lethal pictures of "leading citizens," "successful men of affairs," and "super patriots" placed her solidly among the literary realists at a time when there was both a vogue and a need for them.

Her realism reminds one of Edgar Lee Masters' icy cynicism toward Spoon River's leading "whited sepulchres," but it is counterpoised in her fiction with a deep sympathy toward the unsuccessful, disappointed, inhibited people. She captured the drabness of these lives, forgotten in the backwashes of American bombast. She went further to create amid these gray scenes a faintly mystical tone. This vague mysticism, colored by her characters' private longings for self-assurance, suggests that Zona Gale was not a realist at all. She was, instead, a poet, a mystic, a symbolist. But this deeply flowing, silent strain was not visible to the public's eye or, if seen, not allowed to interfere with its image of her.

III

Before starting *Faint Perfume* (1923), her third and in some ways her best novel explicitly written as realism, she published three minor pieces more interesting for what they imply than for their literary excellence. The first was an inconsequential one-act play for the *Ladies' Home Journal*. Entitled *Uncle Jimmy* (1922), it resurrected for a brief moment the buried Calliope Marsh and her Friendship Village neighbors. That this play should have followed *Miss Lulu Bett* is evidence that Zona Gale's break from Friendship Village sunshine never conclusively occurred. The second piece was the serial *Man at Red Barns*, published in *The Delineator*. Reflecting Zona Gale's growing interest in religious New Thought movements, the novelette's protagonist is John Hazen, a recently widowed Universalist minister who believes that all churches should become one. By preaching universal love, supposedly more deeply infused than any creed, Hazen hopes to eliminate the "stupid duplication or competition of the denominations." Unfortunately, his efforts toward the "evolving process of brotherhood" excite more antipathy than cooperation in the community, the exception being Anita Wentworth who joins him in the double blessedness of both religious reform and matrimony.

In a third work, this time a thin volume of poetry called *The*

Secret Way (1921), Miss Gale again develops what may seem a paradoxical theme for the social reformer who trusts legislation as a means to effect reform. Working assiduously for social legislation, she retains the illusion that any worth-while change must come from within rather than be imposed from without. Her subject in these poems is again love, the secret way to clarify one's sight to "abiding beauty everywhere." In "Contours," she traces beauty as a true line, "drawn from my spirit to some infinite outward place." In "Enchantment," the "ultimate star" becomes her neighbor, and the town's confining walls dissolve like Thoreau's prison.

The interlude, then, between *Miss Lulu Bett* and *Faint Perfume* reveals a deeply moving interest in the metaphysical and a growing crystallization of key ideas soon to be vital. For example, "love" is Zona Gale's term for the release of an indwelling spiritual force fusing with an all-encircling Spirit. One's captivity, even in small-town realities, is never ultimate so long as one's spirit has not been annihilated. Consequently, her hard little pictures of village life lack the dreadful quality with which a Sartre or a Camus would imbue them: her walls are porous and ultimately nonexistent because one's spirit can never be imprisoned, while those of the Frenchmen remain forever impenetrable.

Searching for the certainty that ultimate reality lies somewhere outside the walls, that it transcends the dreary and mundane workaday world, Zona Gale found herself ready to write another *Birth*. Yet she had not finished outlining the bleakness of the market-place world and its tortuous confinement. Her emphasis in *Faint Perfume* still is on the village's uninspired commonplaceness which, when not allayed, turns its inhabitants into clods. Love someday might enable her new heroine, Leda Perrin, to fly above what Miss Gale called the "labyrinth of the unreal," but for now love's absence consigns Leda to the town, ironically named Prospect. In the town one finds Orrin Crumb's house, where Leda lives, no different from Dwight Deacon's. Both are "violently dedicated to the concrete." The faint perfume of spring is barely perceptible, and then only to Leda, the little boy Oliver, his father Barnaby Powers, and old grandfather Crumb. To all the others, who rule the house and town, "the ground was iron beneath dirty snow."

In this novel Zona Gale's use of symbols reveals a surer hand. The red and awesomely beautiful poinsettia dominates the family table, and its "red eye" is like Dr. Eckleburg's in F. Scott Fitzgerald's *The Great Gatsby*; both silently gape upon the human debris. Before the severity of "red eye's" judgment, Leda, trapped in her cousin's household, feels naked. Here is not the nakedness of Richmiel, her fleshy and worldly-wise cousin, whose "yellow gown unclothed her." Instead, Leda is exposed to her own conscience. She stands guilty; the charge is submission to the prosaic and the ugly. By marrying Barnaby, Richmiel's divorced husband, Leda hopes to atone for her guilt: a marriage to another caged spirit would, neatly, liberate both. Barnaby is ideally suited to rescue Leda. No longer distracted by the heavy eyes and wanton ankles of Richmiel, he discovers to his surprise that looking upon Leda reminds him of angels who perhaps "know something better."

But any such knowledge of bliss possessed by angels or by D. H. Lawrence's Miriams will not be Leda's. Earth-bound Richmiel stands in the way. Legally divorced from Barnaby but given custody of their small son Oliver, Richmiel now manipulates him as a pawn to keep Barnaby and Leda apart. Richmiel's heartless game is to allow Barnaby, who adores Oliver, to have his son only as long as Leda remains apart. In this way Richmiel, a hedonist who cares nothing for Oliver, can twist the screw into her former husband and at the same time revenge her jealousy of Leda. Barnaby must choose between rescuing Leda from the Crumbs or freeing Oliver from his mother. His departure with Oliver leaves Leda stranded with only the small hope that someday Richmiel will marry another man, be glad to rid herself legally of the boy, and thereby enable Leda to join with Barnaby.

In the meantime, Leda lives amid all the frustrations and hypocrisies present in Zona Gale's transformed village. Orrin Crumb is stamped from the same machine of Babbittry, and Miss Gale's scalpel cuts just as deftly into the fat as did Lewis'. Busy as both a salesman and Gideonite, Crumb distributes his wares and Bibles with equal gusto: "It would not matter what the *corps* was, the *esprit* would be there." The particularly handy combination he created for himself—the religious order of traveling salesmen—pleases him completely. Cloddish and gauche, he resolves any problem with a grunt, guffaw, sigh, or moral platitude. His wife, Tweet, is just as inert to complexities, except for family intricacies such as Richmiel's divorce which may provoke town gossip. Tweet's two sisters, Richmiel and Pearl, and their mother, lock the cage around Leda.

After Barnaby and Oliver have left, the only kindred but also trapped spirit remaining is grandfather Crumb, a worn-out old man still harboring the feelings of a poet. His last years in his son's household have cost him his privacy and singular dignity. His silence serves as his only refuge. But Richmiel's meanness and the taunting of the others who scorn his old age finally overwhelm him. His suicide note reads: "Canal. By the cottonwood. Blind in a year. Can't take care of my room much longer. Have broken the water picher [sic]. Good bye all. Good bye Leda. Shiny quarters for the little chap."

Swept by desolation now even more profound than that in the valley of ashes named Prospect, Leda sees life as only "cadaver, skeleton, dust." She hears screams inside her which she cannot openly voice to Crumb: "You have killed me a hundred times since I have been in this house. Your way of life is death. I cannot die anymore." Barnaby's remembered words about love and freedom—the faint perfume—provide only fragile solace to Leda who, as the novel ends, sits in the Crumb house which is filled with grandfather's funeral flowers and listens to the hollow voice of Orrin Crumb, the Gideonite: ". . . a Bible in every hotel room. And on the inside cover these wholesome references: If lonesome, read Twenty-third Psalm. If in trouble, read John fourteen. If trade is poor, read——."

Faint Perfume swiftly compresses Zona Gale's distinguishing marks as a literary realist. In this novel her small town again shuts in small people whose cherished values kill spontaneity, imagination, freedom, and life. Ensnared is the fragile soul, like a butterfly, seeking egress. If escape is possible at all, the passage out is as precarious as Thoreau found it to be on leaving the village for Walden Pond. Not only the village's commitment to mercantilism but its intolerance and militant conformity crush a beautiful spirit. Marshall and Jeffrey Pitt, Lulu Bett, Leda Perrin are similar spirits, impaled and imprisoned by Mencken's *boobus americanus.*

Her taut realism—her depressive pictures of American life

etched with bold hard lines—added to the baleful cry, uttered by other realists, that the bumptious *nouveau riche* had left the nation barren of culture. Mark Twain's *The Gilded Age* (1873) and William Dean Howells' *The Rise of Silas Lapham* (1885) and, by the end of the century, more than sixty other novels[20] lampooned the bustling, business-minded, self-satisfied middle class and its new wealth. In 1896 historian Brooks Adams declared in the last chapter of his sensational *Law of Civilization and Decay* that no art can flourish in "the arid modern soil." Critics Van Wyck Brooks, V. F. Calverton, and Matthew Josephson added their voices to the protest. Across the ocean Matthew Arnold had warned against what he called "philistinism," and Swinburne, Wells, Shaw, and Wilde reiterated his warnings. Exile from middle-class mediocrity sent artists to their separate sanctuaries; the Americans in the 1920's were going to Parisian bistros. Zona Gale stayed in Portage and found her escape in contemplating the real mysteries of the river seen from her second-floor back window.

After the last touch of poison in *Faint Perfume* she went no further. She knew she was on the verge of something big, and, whatever it was, it did not lie in further depicting the hollow Deacons and Crumbs nor the broken wings of Lulu and Leda beating empty air. Her literary stature she thought secure, and she was corroborated by such critics as Carl Van Doren who, as fiction editor of *Century Magazine*, told her of his pleasure in serializing *Faint Perfume*, which was followed after its last installment by Willa Cather's three-part novel *The Lost Lady*.[21] Even Heywood Broun, in the New York *World* (March 23, 1923), praised *Faint Perfume*. Edith Wharton's "grumble" that sensitive Leda could not possibly also be a Crumb cousin, elicited from Zone Gale only a quiet answer, not an argument. With something else on her mind, she merely thanked her for the letter and added that she had learned a great deal from writing the book. In a cryptic conclusion she referred to "a certain brooding hope which leaves me quite breathless."[22] That brooding hope concerned her next novel, *Preface to a Life*.

CHAPTER 5

Beyond Realism

I

ONE MAY VIEW Zona Gale's work from several angles. In both her literary and non-literary writing she stepped forth as a social reformer to argue that the government's responsibility included protection not only of property rights but of human rights as well. To this end she supported such causes as women's suffrage, social welfare legislation, Progressive political platforms, and pacifism. As a literary person, she established a solid reputation in both drama and fiction. Her stark realism placed her in company with other Middle West writers protesting against the disruption of the agrarian ideal. Still other facets show her as one widely cognizant of the complexities in national and cultural life unique to the troubled 1920's. Prohibition, new sexual and marriage mores, the debates between science and religion, the *nouveau riche's* "boobocracy," civil liberties, isolationism, and the awesomely patriotic American Legion and Ku Klux Klan—all these controversial aspects swirled around her and frequently colored her work.

In her next novel, *Preface to a Life* (1926), she clearly, if not too explicitly, injects her deep interest in mysticism and its many occult ramifications. This was still another side to her which again illustrates not only her involvement in postwar controversies but also dramatically uncovers her own ambivalence between a social and spiritual orientation. Not surprising is her admission that starting in 1919 her reading, virtually daily, was in either sociology or mysticism. On the six shelves extending across one whole wall of her room she had the books of Anthony Comstock (an American reformer who died in 1915), Lester Ward, and Thorstein Veblen. The mystics were there too: "I lift mine eyes as I write and look upon Gandhi and Ouspensky."[1]

Various causes account for Zona Gale's mystical bent. The broadest one was the new respectability given philosophic idealism at the end of the nineteenth century. Reaction had set in against the apparent non-spiritual, arid outlook of the scientists who had undermined earlier notions held sacrosanct by scriptural and cultural authority. Darwin and Huxley, Comte and Spencer, Pavlov and Freud, Galton and Frazer were but a few such scientists who, embracing their empirical method, had seemed to offer startling proof that life was, as Hippolyte Taine said, a wonderful "mechanical problem." With such terms as "natural selection," "biochemical processes," "conditioned reflex," "Archae-ozoic Age," they created a new scientific world-view founded on an unyielding mechanical determinism. Against this view the nineteenth-century idealists, led by Berkeley and Kant, carried their battle. They held that the world is governed not by blind physical forces but by spiritual ones; that the naturalistic world of physical force and matter was only the world of appearance hiding the real world—the world of mind and spirit.

In America Emerson's philosophy of transcendentalism rein-forced these assertions about the primacy of spirit. By mid-century his followers in St. Louis, calling themselves Neo-Hegelians, set the stage for the New Thought movement which in subsequent years led to Christian Science and the widespread popularity of Theosophy, Spiritualism, other occult groups, and psychical research. Visits to America by such Eastern mystics as Gurdjieff, Krishnamurti, Madame Blavatsky, Grand Duke Alexander of Russia, and Tagore excited further interest in the mystic potencies of life and spirit.

When Zona Gale wrote *Birth* she was irrevocably intrigued by occultism. Long before her, other American writers had professed a similar fascination. Orestes Brownson and Margaret Fuller were active inquirers; Hawthorne and Emerson for a time were eager to learn about it; Henry James in "Professor Fargo" (1874), Oliver Wendell Holmes in *Elsie Venner* (1861), Edward Bellamy in *Looking Backward* (1888), and Howells in *The Undiscovered Country* (1880), *The Shadow of a Dream* (1890), and *Questionable Shapes* (1903), were all concerned with some form of occultism. Edwin Arnold's *Light in Asia* (1879), which told in verse the life and beliefs of an Indian prince who had solved the problems of evil, went through some sixty editions in England

and eighty in the United States. To many Americans Eastern mysticism and, more specifically, Buddhism, offered the answer to a materialistic world and its new sciences. William Sturgis Bigelow wrote *Buddhism and Immortality* (1908); Percival Lowell, *The Soul of the Far East* (1888), John La Farge, who fled to the South Seas and Japan with Henry Adams in 1890, *An Artist's Letters from Japan* (1897); and Lafcadio Hearn, a long series of volumes dealing with Japan, where he had exiled himself.

Added to this speculation came Albert Einstein's theory of relativity, proving the inadequacy of both classical mathematics and Newtonian physics to deal with a surd or irrational universe. His term "relativity" freed the mind of absolutes about fixed time and space. The extreme subjectivism which resulted from such a theory accounted for Claude Bragdon's query, "Are we on the point of discovering that the only reality is thought— consciousness?"[2] P. D. Ouspensky carried subjectivism even further by declaring in *Tertium Organum* (1920) that through "higher consciousness" one can see beyond the three-dimensional world of spatial and limited objects. Other interpretations given to Einstein's theory found in it a refutation of materialism. Einstein, it was said, had shown that matter could be converted into nonmateriality, into energy, a notion giving impressive support to religious groups claiming that matter was in fact immaterial, or, in the words of Mary Baker Eddy, "There is no life, truth, intelligence, nor substance in matter."[3] Sir Oliver Lodge, one of many English occultists who lectured in America during the 1920's, asserted in 1924 that there is "more than a hint" that the electrons "are essentially resolvable into ethereal energy."[4] Alfred North Whitehead's Lowell Lectures in the mid-1920's, published as *Science and The Modern World* (1925), stressed a philosophy of nature as organic rather than materialistic, as function rather than entity.

The point to be made is that the subjective mind was gaining dominion over matter, which in its three-dimensional definition was to many thinkers an inadequate reality. According to Carl Jung in *Modern Man in Search of a Soul* (1933), the "outer world" of matter offered nothing of the psychic life people sought; this trend, said Jung, explained the growth of Spiritualism and Theosophy. Gerald Heard's *These Hurrying Years* (1934), which surveyed the first three decades of the twentieth century, pointed to telepathy as the significant discovery of the 1920's. To Frederick J. Hoffman, "the agony of a spiritual quest in a world that regarded spiritual matters with indifference was one of the most profound emotional experiences of the 1920s."[5]

Zona Gale's seriousness about these matters explains her persistent conviction that only through "higher consciousness"—love, spiritual awakening, freedom of soul—can a person know the "something more" found in her favorite refrain: life is something more than what we think it to be. Convinced that this supra-consciousness required no creeds, no confessions, no dogmas, no denominations, she castigated conventional religion and its, to her, meaningless paraphernalia. She saw it as merely another middle-class custom replete with its own set of obtruding proprieties. Religious faith to her was contingent upon a quickening, a raising of existence to a new level of consciousness.

This new existence would supposedly lead to a new kind of man capable of transcending space and time, mortality and death. Intimations of this new "being" were already evident to persons who had freed themselves from a materialistic worldview. Such persons, she thought, were those sympathetic to the beliefs of the Unitarians, Universalists, and Theosophists. Regardless of organizational differences in each, she regarded them all as efforts to explicate divine essence and its force in the phenomenal universe. From John Haynes Holmes's Unitarian pulpit in New York, she preached on such topics as the birth of the psyche, supernatural revelation, and religious universalism. She wrote for both *The Universalist Leader* and *Unity*, the latter a widely circulated publication which in 1895 had merged with *Christian Science Thought*, itself a descendant of Mrs. Eddy's *Christian Science Journal*. As for the Theosophists, she explained to Frank Miller of Mission Inn, California, that she was intrigued with their attitude that the present, or "Fifth," great race is being destroyed to give rise to the "Sixth"—the "new species" as Ouspensky called it. She followed with keen attention Mrs. Annie Besant, successor to Madame Blavatsky as international head of the Theosophical Society, who went to Ojai, California, in 1926 to supervise this newly gathered "species" in the name of Theosophy.

The whole New Thought movement, seeking to deduce

spiritual force in all matter, generally held to the efficacy of this force in improving human existence. Adherents, including Zona Gale, sought to establish a universal brotherhood of humanity. Along with the "social gospel" theorists, she believed that, since all men are brothers, all the problems of life, including those of economics and international affairs, would be finally solved if only people could be persuaded to love one another, or, in different words, to reach a higher consciousness. Zona Gale's pacifism was rooted in this idea. The temptation to regard this notion as sentimentality cannot be resisted if one thinks of the recalcitrance of human nature, expressed in St. Paul's oft-quoted confession, "The good that I would do, I do not do; and the evil that I would not, that I do." A modern Paul would find the power of positive thinking unappealing and inadequate; Zona Gale's reply would be her statement written for *Unity* (July 27, 1925): "There is more to be known of our power of participation than was known to Paul." "Know ye not," she hortatively adds, "that ye are daily in creative consonance with the Central Life—in *consonance*."

Also in accordance with the New Thought movement, she studied the religion and philosophy of the East. One of her favorite interpreters of Orientalism was L. Adams Beck whose mass of writing included such titles as *The Ninth Vibration* (1922), *The Perfume of the Rainbow* (1923), *The Splendour of Asia: the Story and Teaching of the Buddha* (1926). Evelyn Underhill's *Mysticism* (1911) took her to the *Bhagavad-Gita* and to the writings of Meister Eckhart. Equally impressive to her were Walt Whitman's raging lines and the limpid writing of Rabindranath Tagore, a Hindu poet whose mystical idealism and gentle arraignment of Western civilization threaded such volumes as *Gitanjali* (1912), *Songs of Kabir* (1915), *Creative Unity* (1922), and *Fireflies* (1928).

Still other works to which she often referred in correspondence were Benjamin Kidd's *The Science of Power* (1918) with its emphasis upon a new "psychic centre of power" (especially in the mind of woman) as an antidote to "the failure of Western knowledge"; J. D. Buck's *Cosmic Consciousness* (1920), full of case studies of those who had entered into cosmic consciousness; and Robert Courtney's *Beyond Behaviorism* (1927), whose opening description of the psyche Zona Gale compared with the development of the butterfly: from a larva to "aerial life" and thence escape from the *cul de sac* of "mechanically habitized action."[6]

Most sensational of New Thought efforts was the investigation of a person's mystic and extrasensory capacities. Of course mystic inquiry vastly antedates its American equivalent. But a strange chapter in American literary history could be written about certain realists—say from Howells on—whose interests in the spirit world as opposed to the grimly material one led them into captivating inquiries about professional mediums, mystics, spiritualists, and psychical researchers. In *Forty Years of Psychic Research* (1936) and *The Mystery of the Buried Crosses: A Narrative of Psychic Exploration* (1939) Hamlin Garland documented his long-time psychical interests which had begun when he wrote *The Tyranny of the Dark* (1905) and *The Shadow World* (1908). Upton Sinclair, famous for his fiercely naturalistic novel *The Jungle* (1906), conducted experiments in mental telepathy and reported them in *Mental Radio* (1930). Theodore Dreiser, another writer reaching beyond materialistic chaos, contemplated the spirit world not only of Divine Love but, as he writes in *Dawn* (1931), of telepathy and premonition: "How is it that this is still denied—long-distance sensitivity to important occurrences?"[7]

Higher or cosmic consciousness, telepathy, precognition, spiritualism—what it all comes to, as Rosalind Heywood tells in *Beyond the Reach of Sense* (1961), is the belief that a man can make contact with distant events or with supra-phenomena by an unknown process not involving sight, hearing, touch, taste, or smell. Such miraculous inventions as the telegraph and telephones further beckoned people's curiosities about thought transmission, especially between the living and the "dead." Thomas A. Edison tried for awhile to make "a sort of valve" to allow "personalities in another existence" to have a "better opportunity to express themselves than the tilting tables and raps and ouija boards and mediums and other crude methods now purported to be the only means of communication."[8] The year before Edison announced his intention, Francis Grierson devised what he called a "psychophone" to use during his lectures given to the Toronto Theosophical Society in 1919. This "phone," instrumenting intercourse between this world and the next, brought in messages which

Grierson recorded in *Psycho-Phone Messages* (1921). Garland boasted that Los Angeles mediums he knew had received messages from the spirits of Henry James, Sir Arthur Conan Doyle, Walt Whitman, and others. Edith Ellis in *Open the Door* (1935) reported contact with Madame Blavatsky, Abraham Lincoln, the Virgin Mary, and Jesus Christ!

II

Knowing the peculiar matrix nurturing Zona Gale's own occultism helps to account for the divided stream in her writing—the dull ordinary world and the strange land of spirit. Just before she began writing *Preface to a Life* an extremely important event occurred, sending her further adrift into the spirit world: the death of her mother.

The closeness of mother and daughter appears early in Miss Gale's letters. Overwhelming evidence that Miss Gale wished the relationship unbroken was her delay in accepting Ridgely Torrence's proposal of marriage which he later withdrew. Through the years she stayed close to her mother, assuring her each time she went to New York or elsewhere that she would not remain away long. When Eliza Gale died on May 29, 1923, Zona Gale lost not only her anchor in life but also, to her, the apotheosis of human life in its spiritual richness. For several months afterwards she was grief-stricken; her friends remember this time as the only occasion when Zona Gale ever was seen lacking self-control.

To the many friends who expressed condolence she sent a reply addressed "Dear Friends" and signed "C. F. Gale and Zona Gale." In it she wrote of motherhood as a correspondence to "some profound spiritual order, but faintly felt on earth." She saw her mother as symbolic of some mystery "in which we share," some "Mother Principle" which, as she later expressed to Dorothy Canfield Fisher, is the root of life.[9] In her Friendship Village stories she intimated the presence of such an extraphysical force. With her own mother's death came the chance to validate not only their closeness but, within this principle, their mystical oneness.

She recorded hundreds of "spirit messages" sent by her mother from the next world. Most of them are illegible, undecipherable.

Automatic writing as practiced by psychics in a trance supposedly was to appear only dimly intelligible because of the remoteness from whence the messages came. This fact explains Zona Gale's strangely serpentine handwriting as she slowly traced out, for example, her mother's words: "I'm snuggled down in you Dumb baby. But take me & hold me & keep me always. I'll love you will ever & ever & ever Amen." Another transcription: "You little soul I near, nearer, nearly all the time. I no more gone than you are & not so much. I live—I b'lieve it! I breathe different. That's all & better. Hold my hands, hold my hands—all the time. O Blessed. Be me or I you, Darling child. Yet, Yet—I feel you."[10]

In death Eliza Gale authenticated what in life she had mysteriously appeared to her daughter to be: one through whom a divine intelligence passed. Zona Gale remembered that, with the coming of death, her mother grew more clairvoyant. She would stand before a Madonna picture and "speak with tongues, in a sort of inspired might." Miss Gale remembered that her mother sometimes would punctuate weird, dream-like stories which she told her with the words, "And the sun was shining & I was young," referring to the astral light and to eternal youth.[11]

The relationship of mother and daughter allegedly culminated in a mystical union overcoming the finiteness of both. The social or community "shutupness" with its corollary in mortality itself now dissolved in the fulfillment of spirit. This fulfillment becomes Zona Gale's escape from the world of ordinary trivialities, as oppressive to her as to her fictional personages caught in small-town bleakness.

If from all this one ventures to hypothesize about Miss Gale's psychological state—her frustration, say, and her need to sublimate certain drives or to palliate guilt—one could imagine a Kafkaesque portrayal with *maternal* authority at its all-ruling center. Or one could lightly dismiss her whole quest for astral reality as the fad of an occultist. That there were those like Zona Gale who did sincerely desire freedom from the incubus of materialism and triviality through the New Thought is a fact not taken lightly by George Santayana who, in *Character and Opinion in the United States* (1920), saw nothing incredible in a person's using means—even spirit messages—to discover some cosmic or inner energy not hitherto at the disposal of man. Certainly for the student of literature nothing is extraneous which may shed light upon an author's work, especially when—as with Zona Gale—the spirit world is basic to her total literary design.

III

Preface to a Life takes its protagonist, Bernard Mead, up to that astral plane allegedly the next one above the tangible world. His small-town neighbors think him mad, but such is the price the mystic pays. Often, like a revenant, only his mother understands his madness. Her prophetic words about death and life annoy all but Bernard who, slowly, fathoms in them a haunting wisdom. The two grow spiritually closer until, near death, old Mrs. Mead comforts Bernard by saying: "I'm going to carry you—just like I did before—till you get born again. . . . You didn't know I was round you before. Why'll you know this time." With eyes shut Mrs. Mead sees *her* mother—"I've thought about her all day"—and then whispers to Bernard, "She and I'll look after you. She'll carry me and I'll carry you." Swept by the thought that his own mother symbolically represented "infinitudes of mothers," Bernard watches her nearing death as one "moving, shining, flowing into light, light of the Godhead" which illumines the cosmic womb. To Bernard, Zona Gale's oedipal explanation of the Mother Principle, written in a later essay, is now being enacted: "The word mother has a correspondence in nature, beyond the individual and beyond the possessive. This word seems to signify some spiritual condition which is to the macrocosm what she is to the human atom."[12] To him, God was maternal, Her cosmos a womb, and every mother microcosmic.

Critics reading the novel did not touch upon this key to its interpretation. They read it as a study of Bernard Mead's struggle to orient his inner life, not as autobiography describing the author's psychical pilgrimage to her mother's spirit world and furthermore, not as Zona Gale's most daring exploration into spiritism. They noticed, however, that she had attempted more than Lewis had done with Babbitt, whose generic incapacity to grasp structural and spiritual meanings limited him to his bourgeois treadmill. Her work more closely resembles Willa Cather's *The Professor's House*, published a year earlier; Professor St. Peter, like Bernard Mead, seeks meaning beyond the thick layer of materialism, but at the price of social ostracism.

Bernard Mead's treadmill was first his lumber business, the prosperity of which was determined by the number of trees it destroyed; then his trivial wife Laura, whom he married instead of the more imaginative Alla; and finally his strategy for maintaining Pauquette respectability. What he thought to be perfect contentment was instead perfect submission to "the bitch goddess Success" which disastrously led to psychic lethargy and then to complete bondage. Like the miracle of spring, his spirit finally rebels not against Pauquette but his own numbness. He begins to notice beauty and strangeness in everything around him, as if they uncovered a loveliness which he had never seen on his treadmill. With this extension of consciousness, a fourth dimension of motion opens to Mead so that whatever he sees is multiplied in motion: "the grass, the trees, the air, the sky, all blowing and beating and seeming to him not one scene, but manifold greens and skies, all in swinging, ordered motion, and standing out with the clarity of fire."

Zona Gale claimed to have had similar experiences of her own. To her friend Alice Bailey she confided that during some of her "meditations"—while completing her manuscript of *Preface to a Life*—she had instantaneously slipped "into the farther field of consciousness." At these times visualized objects changed into a "mass of form, airy, indescribable."[13] The account reminds one of Van Gogh's swirling trees or D. H. Lawrence's pulsating gardens, but its antecedent was more likely the movement called Futurism, started in 1909 by Filippo Tommaso Marinetti whose manifesto called for a "complete renewal of human sensibility."[14] He wanted artists to see into the movement of things, just as scientists had discovered such invisible activity in electricity. The Futurist painters then would supposedly *see* a halo if they chose to paint one. Excitedly following the manifesto, Zona Gale explained that Futurists recaptured "that which lies within some other area of form than that form to which we are accustomed."[15]

Bernard Mead, like a Futurist artist, could actually see what the scientists found true about the motion of all matter. "I've got microscopes in my eyes," he jubilantly cries to everyone. "Currents in the chair, in the cushion, in the air—we live the whole time in a whirlpool and never know it." And, like Whitman, what he saw he became. But his new sense of wonder only means to his village and family that he is insane. Called by Laura Mead, Dr. McCormick asks his patient the routine questions. Father and grandfather living? Alone a good deal? Any outlets? He casually brings in such terms as hysterics and convulsions, infantilism, epilepsy. His final verdict is insanity: "an uncommon case."

Bernard goes to Alla in whose garden he had earlier experienced his first contact with vibrant nature. Desperately hopeful that she will understand, he recounts how something within him had sickened from feeding too much on "lumber and coffee and bacon and talk." Exclaiming that he had "escaped into something real . . . all motion, beautiful motion," he suddenly pauses, only to hear her flippant reply, "That's ridiculous." She too believes him insane. He returns home to the six women who are dependents there and takes up his task of living on. But he tightly holds to himself the only ray of light that he has ever known: that life may not be the treadmill that he had thought it to be, that it has another aspect. He calls to his mother who replies, "Little more courage down here. Little more love." If he can draw down courage and love, he can link himself with the life he guesses to be inside of life; then—at fifty-two—he will begin to live. The treadmill will remain, to be sure. But he knows that it has something more, even though he can make no one else know it.

Though not knowledgeable about the deeply autobiographical significance of the novel, readers warmly responded to it despite its awkwardly integrated philosophy. During its first year booksellers sold more copies of it than of *Miss Lulu Bett*. Mencken would have run it in his *American Mercury* if a precedent against serials had not existed.[16] Reviewers Samuel Chew and Louis Kronenberger praised it highly, both suggesting that Bernard represents the only authentic sanity.[17] More recently, Frederick Hoffman has called the book "fabulous."[18] An important observation made by W. J. Blyton who traced idealism in recent fiction applies to Zona Gale at this point: a wider realism must do justice to a vastly important "dream-life" running contemporaneously with our prosaic "event-life."[19]

Her realism was "wider" than Sinclair Lewis'. More like that of Sherwood Anderson and Willa Cather, its mystical overtones as in *Preface to a Life* bring new dimensions to the humdrum life of Bernard Mead. When they are absent, life becomes the wasteland of the Crumbs or the Deacons. Not satisfied as mere observers piling up details and externals, realists like Zona Gale searched for this "something more." "I am the despair of my orthodox materialistic friends," said Upton Sinclair, "because I insist upon believing in the possibility of so many strange things."[20] Dreiser's second wife, Helen, insisted that no matter how realistic his books were, "Dreiser was a mystic, first, last, and always."[21] For all its realism, John Steinbeck's *Grapes of Wrath* also rests on an Emersonian mystique.

Nothing else Zona Gale wrote has the bursting, vertiginous style found in *Preface to a Life*. A long novel, second only to *Birth*, its language is profusely and often uncontrollably sensuous. Like an unweeded garden, its plants gone wild, her descriptions suggest a heightened awareness of everything. Cascades of imagery in page-long paragraphs create a tone throbbing with the same molecular energy as that being depicted. Inevitably, after the flurry of words has subsided, the reader discovers the language has been too extravagant, too pyrotechnic.

The novel, however, must be considered one of her major works. It marks her farthest excursion into the mystical; and, when placed alongside *Miss Lulu Bett* and *Faint Perfume*, it once again establishes the tension between the mundane and the spiritual first attempted in *Birth*. It also stands as a private account of the author's effort to fortify her own inner self, the only escape from Portage. To be in and out at the same time was Zona Gale's paradox; maintaining an equipoise was her private agony.

Ironically, as with other contemporaries who were also bewildered by their own divided stream, her literary success and reputation grew from the materials of the prosaic world which her temperament was disinclined to accept. Her slices of realistic life strike a tone of authenticity; her spirituality rings hollow. Attempting to reach into the vastness of both psychology and theology, she fails in her fiction to capitalize upon the tension between the real and the spiritual. To show both the complexity and drama of this ambivalence was her artistic as well as philosophical problem. She wanted to picture real life but she wanted "something more" too. Instead of Portage serving as a symbol of real life—which her readers accepted—she tried to show in *Birth* and in *Preface to a Life* that Portage people were something more. But she failed to make that added dimension credible. To Marcel Proust, Joyce, or Faulkner that "something" would have been what Henry James called "the atmosphere of the mind," the chamber in which all the fugitive thoughts are caught and all time *is*. To Kafka it would have been all the teleological ambiguities shrouding the Castle.

Of course Zona Gale could hardly be expected to stand next to these giants. But the extent to which she failed to understand the deeper complexities, the something more, of both man and God indicates the distance separating her from these literary masters who were also her contemporaries. In short, her ambivalent wavering led to excellent sketches of ordinary life but to one-sided platitudes about the supra-ordinary. Consequently, as characters, Marshall Pitt is less than tragic and Bernard Mead less than sublime. The glass through which her own world-view unfolded was foggier than she supposed.

IV

Several years passed before Zona Gale attempted anything again like *Preface to a Life*. In the meantime her study in eastern mysticism continued. Claude Bragdon, himself a student of mysticism, kept her regularly informed about such matters as his New York visits with Krishnamurti and Gurdjieff. Her fascination with the latter's institute at Fontainebleau (where Katherine Mansfield, A. R. Orage, and Ouspensky studied for a time) led to a subscription to his home-study course. At this time too she met Francis Grierson, the aging psycho-phonist, and also Frank Miller whose esoteric interests in Mission Inn provided material for a later book.

A letter she wrote to Socialist Norman Thomas reveals her wish to subordinate public issues to this higher quest of spirit. Written in 1926, the year of *Preface to a Life*, it makes clear the tenacity and permanence of the newer spiritual claims. She said she was becoming more "non-resistant all the time" toward issues foremost to the Socialist party. "I can see perfectly well," she went on, "how strikes and social conflict is [*sic*] the way by which certain expression must be found and certain advances made. But I know better every year that these are not my way.

I believe that there is a release of spiritual force which is hampered by any form of conflict however carried on. . . . But whether or not I am wrong, this seems to be now the truth for me."[22]

Even though steadfast as a spiritual visionary, she did not soften the tones of her realism. *Preface to a Life* was an exception, an important one. But she still considered herself committed to what Faulkner has called one's "own little postage stamp of native soul." Far as Zona Gale wandered into psychical realms, Portage remained her native soil and its people her own. *Yellow Gentians and Blue* (1927) attests to this severe localism.

She wrote the short stories in this collection while she was working on *Preface to a Life,* and several of them were first published in *Collier's* and *Century Magazine.* Dealing with the most commonplace happenings of undistinguished, small-town people, they are divided into two parts: (1) those belonging to the "yellow gentians" and taking their quality from the bitter taste attributable to the roots of this flower; (2) those belonging to the "blue gentians" which, to the author, supposedly push "through from some inner place of being." It is significant that Zona Gale grouped by far the greater number of these stories with the yellow gentians.

The stories, skillfully etched vignettes, are like a prose *Spoon River Anthology.* Futility and death are common themes. In "The Charivari" the curiosity and heckling of neighbors drive Obald to his death. "Autobiography" is written as an account of an immigrant wife's disenchantment with America; her arduous ocean journey causes the death of her little daughter. A carpenter in "Bill," dying of tuberculosis, finds someone to adopt his six-year-old motherless daughter who, as she leaves his house, forgets to wave her hand. "Last Night" ends with the obituary notice: "The dead body of an unknown man was found in the scale house at the stockyard, where he had been making his home while he peddled needles and pencils about the town." In "Bella" a headstone is significantly absent from a certain grave. "Cherries" merely tells the story of Nellie who "married the chief banker of the town, had a beautiful home and an idiot son."

Two stories stirred more than routine interest. Edward J. O'Brien included "The Biography of Blade" in his edition of *Best Stories of 1924,* and two years later he chose "Ernie Mendenhall" for a companion edition. The first of these stories again caused commotion when *Liberty*, a nickel weekly magazine, published in its August 16, 1930, issue Parker Bloser's plagiarized version entitled "The Biography of Loar." Zona Gale pressed no charges, but she saw the incident receive full coverage in *Time*[23] and in Maurice Salsman's book, *Plagiarism: The "Art" of Stealing Literary Material* (1931).

Yellow Gentians and Blue was Zona Gale's sixteenth book of fiction. Her output up to 1928 also included poetry collected in *The Secret Way*; four plays—*The Neighbors, Miss Lulu Bett, Uncle Jimmy,* and *Mister Pitt* (1925), the latter an adaptation of *Birth;* incidental, uncollected magazine stories; and essays on social and political topics. That year she brought out her first collection of essays which, as pieces on literary theory, comprise an important synthesis of what she thought the significance of her craft to be.

CHAPTER 6

Theory and Practice

I

TWENTY-TWO YEARS after Zona Gale wrote her first novel she collected seven important essays from among many previously published, wrote four additional ones, and published all eleven, along with two book reviews, as *Portage, Wisconsin and Other Essays* (1928). These carefully arranged selections constitute an apologia for her entire literary output up to 1928.

The first group—two essays about Portage and one each about her father and mother—describes the tight little world where she lived and wrote. The second group contains her remaining essays, arranged to show the evolution of her literary intent. All together, the essays designate 1928 as a milestone for Zona Gale, a time for stock-taking and looking back at the road long traveled. They summarize what her literary aims had been and point the direction in which, in her opinion, literature must go.

Those in the second group require special attention, for they constitute her specific effort to synthesize the literary theories she conceived and practiced. Opening this group with her essay, "United States and the Artist," she attacks head-on the question: Can an artist exist and function freely in the United States? Cooper, Irving, Hawthorne, James, and Henry Adams had asked and, in their separate ways, had acted upon this question in the nineteenth century; to the same question during Zona Gale's day American literary exiles from the Left Bank in Paris were thunderously answering "No!" Her own answer was "Yes," but it was neither loud nor confident. Because of what she called "the disabilities of this country as a garden for his growth," the American artist choosing to stay at home would survive, she said, only by freeing himself from the "prejudice and standardization" surrounding him. While writing, he must become "independent of the State," especially when it demands, as does America, that the artist should first prove himself able to make a solid living before he has a right to follow his artistic fancies. If he successfully resists cultural hostility toward art, then he can choose his spot to work. Zona Gale said that for her, "it should be a small Middle Western town—it should be Portage, Wisconsin—with a lawn running down to a river. . . ."

But what of those writers who claimed that regardless of the artist's independence, he would still find himself stifled in America? Edith Wharton and Zona Gale debated this subject in long correspondence. Miss Wharton, in London, took the position, later summarized in the *Yale Review*,[1] that the great American novel would never be about Main Street, contrary to the success Sinclair Lewis was enjoying. Her point was that the stuff of art does not come from "a safe, shallow and shadowless world"—America. With its "dead level of prosperity and security" and its absence of "nicely shaded degrees of culture and conduct," the only subject matter remaining for the novelists is "just folks" and the flat surfaces of their democratic towns—unless, of course, one goes outside the "American 12-mile limit" as did Poe and Melville. She argued much like her London companion, Henry James, who had earlier noted in his 1879 essay on Hawthorne that "a large juvenility" stamped itself on America; its towns were merely "large, respectable, prosperous, and democratic." Hawthorne himself lamented in his Preface to *The Marble Faun* that instead of shadows, antiquities, and mysteries, America could boast of only "a commonplace prosperity, in broad and simple daylight." The same complaint goes back to Cooper, who as early as 1828 in *Notions of the Americans,* asserted that he "had never seen a nation so alike" as the people in the United States.

Zona Gale acknowledged America's lack of cultural depth, the absence of the ordered and the mellow, of echoes and memories. "But who of the Pilgrims," she asked in this same essay, "regretted that their meeting house in the woods lacked a nave or a transept?" Art interprets life "whatever life may be."

From Miss Gale's standpoint the American artist had to keep himself independent from designs the public might try to impose upon his work. Most important to reject was sentimentality. She argued that the writer's new responsibility was to shun the romantic for the realistic, "to face folk and life, even at the cost of idols and illusions."[2] She stood squarely against the sentimentalists; and from her revolt against the Kathleen Norrises and the Gene Stratton-Porters, and also against her own early Friendship Village period, came *Miss Lulu Bett* and *Faint Perfume* as well as generous praise for the work of Stephen Crane, Theodore Dreiser, Sinclair Lewis, and, in lavish abundance, for the Middle Border novels of Hamlin Garland.[3]

As she tried so openly to demonstrate in *Preface to a Life,* she also asserted in her essay "United States and the Artist" that small-town people, despite their lack of cultural density, have a "human spirit." Much like Howells' famous reply to Henry James, who could find no literary materials in a rudimentary social order, Zona Gale would also have answered, "There is the whole of human nature!" Art, she wrote, "seeks to interpret the human spirit, naked in the universe, itself without nationality." At this point she comes close to the necessary distinction between "romantic" and "romance." "Romantic" she rejected as sentimental. But as Hawthorne defined "romance" in his Preface to *The House of the Seven Gables,* this word pertains to "the truth of the human heart." In aiming for truth through literature, Zona Gale wished the little affairs of contemporary life, even though minutely shown, finally to become transparent and to reveal a oneness of all people at all times. Or, in different terms, she aimed to show characters separate from their social or cultural distinctions. Each one stands against the sky, seeking either to come to terms with the universe or to discover a universe within himself.

The artist in the United States, she said, will have no illusions that he is anywhere else but in America. Yet he must not limit his materials to the postage-stamp locality surrounding him. He must create his characters from a broader base—the base of their essential humanness. Like Natty Bumppo, Ahab, or Joe Christmas, they should be larger than their social relevance. While there is, one needs to add, this relevance in the characters of Cooper, Melville, and Faulkner, a recent critic has correctly said that "it's the *unsocial* definition that elevates these authors."[4] Similarly, the "unsocial" dimension of characters in their cosmic relationships was what Zona Gale ultimately sought. She ·saw herself as more than a regional realist. Unfortunately, her grasp was not commensurate with her reach.

II

Her next two essays—"Implications" and "Conversation"—make the singular point that American writing should transcend its native materials. Again she stressed that writers should not limit themselves to regional caricatures. Instead, they should look through the close-at-hand to discover implications behind the habitual. This artistic vision will uncover "the faint inner significance for which few have memory or attention."

She displayed but a shaky understanding of the more *avant-garde* novelists busy with psychological implications. Such names as Faulkner, Hemingway, Joyce, Proust, and Lawrence appear in none of her critical essays. Virginia Woolf was the only radically experimental novelist whose work attracted her; it corroborated her own notion that there is no such thing as inaction. That all is furious motion all the time was impressively illustrated for her by Virginia Woolf's *To a Lighthouse*; she said she "reveled"[5] in all the inner reactions, thoughts, perceptions, memories, involuntary and voluntary mental processes of the half dozen characters in it. Virginia Woolf's employing new forms, including stream of consciousness, in *Mrs. Dalloway* and *Orlando* struck Zona Gale as entirely legitimate means by which to enter into and identify with the beat and roll and the actual atmosphere of things.

Spiritual implications appealed to her more than the underside of consciousness. Her all-important word "implications" suggested the same profundity and led to the same abstractions as Wordsworth's word "intimations." Instead of the stuff of today, she wanted nothing short of spirituality. In practice, however, her obtruding efforts to imbue the regional with astral light vitiated many of her otherwise excellent works.

Her next pair of essays in *Portage, Wisconsin*—"The Novel and the Spirit" and "The Novel of Tomorrow"—advance her point further. But first she reiterates her satisfaction that modern novelists no longer shy away from realism. That they show

"life's sheer deadly death-dealing routine" and the sometimes unpleasant people trapped by its monotony, wholesomely expands
the novelist's range, she believes, beyond the old Anglo-Saxon
limitation of subject matter.

The deficiency is the novelist's "lack of power to express
beauty. Beauty as a force. Inhering beauty. Almost, one adds,
incommunicable beauty." She credited the modern novelists with
showing that "life is not all apples," but their shortcoming was in
supposing that "orchards bear exclusively cores—or even worms."
Discounting her unfortunate image of Eden as a Portage apple
orchard, one detects her basic denial of a tragic vision. Beyond
precept she finds beauty, not chaos. Those persons in her fiction
who go beyond are blessedly done with both temptation and
polemics. Serene in their transformation, they can then begin
"beautiful living." Such living is not a matter of conscious
perfection as sentimentally seen, for example, in the perfect
family relationship or perfect love depicted in a Norman Rock-
well drawing. It is instead a matter of sensing one's "free spirit
within in fleeting union with an exquisite and inexorable spirit
without." Too many artists, she claimed, either wallowed in
sentimentality when treating the spirit or else, turning away
from it completely, found unholy joy in the pathological and
drunken. In either case, they were missing the magic and beauty
of life. Novelists apparently not missing the ambrosia were May
Sinclair, Anne Douglas Sedgwick, and Mary Johnston, whom
Zona Gale recommended to a certain graduate student inquiring
about a subject for a master's thesis. In trying to dissuade her
from writing about her own novels, Zona Gale suggested reading
these other women novelists and writing on the subject, "The
Treatment of Spirit in Modern Fiction."[6]

A cotton-wool fuzziness obscures Zona Gale's exposition about
literature and spiritual reality. Her pivotal point that truth
equals subliminal beauty discounts the equally valid claim that
truth, as in Sartre's *Nausea* or in Leonid Andreyev's "Lazarus,"
may reveal cosmic nothingness. The point is that an aesthetic
dependent upon metaphysical presuppositions, which may or
may not be valid, precludes acceptance of artistic work failing
to corroborate those same presuppositions. To say, as Zona Gale
does in "The Novel of Tomorrow," that the spiritual world served
by art gives "the spell and perfume to the commonplace"

requires first the admission of such a world and, secondly, a knowledge of its nature—to say nothing of its accessibility to man.

Even so, Zona Gale's prediction that the novel of tomorrow will uncover the beauty of our essential commonplace living may have had an uncanny accuracy. The modern novel does reveal beauty, though hardly the kind shaped by serenity and unconscious perfection. Instead of Zona Gale's clairvoyant mother speaking in tongues before a Madonna picture, the most beautiful sight to the novelist may more powerfully be a Sisyphus forever condemned to roll a rock to the top of a mountain and fully conscious of the struggle's tormenting futility. Not by transcending human condition but rather by honestly confronting it as being without divine immanence, the artist may make a more compelling beauty take shape. Because this kind of humanistic beauty exists apart from any supraphenomenal world of spirit, Zona Gale would deny its completeness. Perhaps for just such a reason, her ideas are a world away from today's readers.

To say this is not to imply that twentieth-century novelists eschew metaphysics. The difference between the masters and the Wisconsin novelist on this point is in the texture of the sky before which their heroes stand alone. Zona Gale's is effulgent, exquisite, and hardly comparable to the rain-filled one in Hemingway's *Farewell to Arms*. Her sky in theory is like the one arching Faulkner's Lena Grove in *Light in August* until, nearing Jefferson, Lena sees it spoiled by smoke thinly towering above Joanna Burden's house wherein Miss Burden's almost severed head faces backward. The cosmic terror emblazoning Ahab's corposants or Arthur Dimmesdale's midnight heaven has no equivalent in Zona Gale.

She believed that what contemporary fiction lacked, and what the American novel of tomorrow must have to fulfill its destiny, is her kind of beauty—delicate, lovely, refined, ethereal. She found "bits" of this beauty in Edith Wharton, Howells, James, "and from a half-dozen of the moderns. . . . But not enough beauty." It would seem to the casual student of American literature that there is impressive splendor in Melville, Hawthorne, parts of Mark Twain, much of James, and only a tenuous wisp in blue-stocking novelists like Mary Johnston and Anne Douglas Sedgwick whom Miss Gale recommended. All her talk about beauty tends to make one squirm at her precious-ness. If she had more strongly succeeded in evoking beauty in her fiction, her talk *about* it would seem less offensive and inflated.

About literary technique Miss Gale had little to say even though the critical writings of James, Percy Lubbock, and E. M. Forster were looming as breathtaking precedents. She liked Virginia Woolf's engaging stylistic flux, but she attempted no detailed analysis of it or its contemporary parallels. Her exaspera-tion with the fringed and tasseled style of the sentimentalists inspired no sustained explanation. She merely held that a direct form—"bare and clean as a plain"—best penetrates to the heart of the subject. She thought style should be compact, free from deliberate sordidness which to her was affectation, and, most importantly, saturated "with all that divination can capture of communicable beauty."

III

Concerning the novel of tomorrow, the crisis to Zona Gale was not one of technique or form; it was rather of metaphysics. In this light, the last two essays in *Portage, Wisconsin* crown her achievement in literary criticism.

Underlying both "The Beauty and the Commonplace" and "Scholarship and the Spirit" is her definition of art and the artist. Art, she wrote, "reveals"; it does not invent. It draws beauty down from astral heights—from an Elsewhere of pleasure-domes, one might say—so that the commonplace in manifesting another plane becomes inhabited with "angels." Art goes back not merely to nature but to ideas or forms antecedent to nature. Its intrinsic value, as Thomas Carlyle earlier claimed, lies in its rendering more visible the nature of the godhead which, to Zona Gale, was beauty. Following Carlyle's explanation in his chapter on "Symbols" in Book III of *Sartor Resartus*, one notices that he also thought that in the aesthetic experience man is brought into more or less direct communication with the infinite.

The artist, therefore, is one who by some special grace of see-ing serves as the instrument by which beauty is thus made visible to common man. This special grace Zona Gale described as "a heightening of perception akin to the experience which the East knows as illumination." Presumably, then, practice in writing should be to the novelist what meditation is to the saint. Both have to do with transcendental powers which, though not fully understood, are to be contacted and then appropriated. Clearly, Zona Gale thought the artist to be a mystic and his intimacy with beauty akin to a religious experience. His mysticism would be bound up with aesthetics by giving him an explanation of why he finds art valuable at all and, at the same time, by enabling him through his art to fashion truths of eternal validity and beauty. His mystical or heightened consciousness would transform the ordinary world. Seeing it not as ugly but as inherently beautiful, the artist-mystic, as Emerson said, would see beauty even in a corpse or, in Zona Gale's words, would create a future fiction which "will realize angels in the commonplace."

It is surprising that Zona Gale was not attracted to the French Symbolist poets to whom literature and mysticism were mutually dependent. Faced with a choice between realism and the alluring revival of idealism, they too veered toward mysticism and the supra-world of spirit. Led by Stéphane Mallarmé, they nurtured a deep belief in idealism, "a nostalgia for the past and for a sense of purity and a striving for the absolute."[7]

Equally unaccountable was her lack of attention to music which, at least in Europe at the end of the nineteenth century, was foremost among the arts. Henri Bergson, for example, thought it the most immediate and directly felt of aesthetic forms. Richard Wagner's mystical tones testified to its soaring power. In attempting to spiritualize literature, Mallarmé and his followers spoke in terms of the "instrumentation" of a poem, and they hoped to approximate in words the wonderous indefiniteness of music.[8] Walter Pater in *Giorgione* said that to him "all art aspires toward the condition of music." Yet for all the associations between literature and music, and for all the mystical significance music allegedly carried, Zona Gale displayed little familiarity with it.

Her ultimate concern focused upon sublimation regardless of the means used to attain it. For her final critical essay in *Portage, Wisconsin* she significantly chose "Scholarship and the Spirit," which earlier had appeared as "Allotropes" in the *Yale Review* (January, 1926). In this essay more than in any other she pointed to man's fabulous potentialities, which only artists have the grace of sight to unfold. Her keystone is the word "allotrope," which she defined as "that whose constituents, identical with those of something else, yet have a different molecular arrangement, so that the two present quite different aspects." In other words, an element is allotropic if it has two or more different forms. Thus, a diamond is an allotrope of coal, both formed of the same constituents. The most compelling problem, then, is to discover the allotrope of present-day man. Does he exist in a different form? Zona Gale believed so. "As we creep about in this primordial ooze, with our faint toys of radium and radio and aeroplane, we can begin to dream what they will be perceiving and feeling when finer and fairer allotropes of other things have been discovered: of air, of fire, of earth, of ourselves."

Allotropes of men! This concept is the possibility which—for the Ouspenskys, Blavatskys, and hosts of others—opened the door to a new race of mankind and, better yet, to "the divinization of man." The artists' quest is singularly for allotropes to make clear the fact that behind ordinary things and just plain folks "there is visible a new pattern of the old spiritual treasures." To perceive a different and, supposedly, more beautiful molecular arrangement is, suddenly, to see more man, more thing, more life. At such a moment, when man sees through all, he himself becomes in Emersonian terms a "transparent eyeball," a phenomenon Mark Twain would rather have chosen to describe as seeing "through a glass eye, darkly."

Concluding *Portage, Wisconsin* are "Two Summaries," actually reviews of Robert Courtney's *Beyond Behaviorism: The Future of Psychology* (1927) and Denis Saurat's *The Three Conventions: Metaphysical Dialogues* (1926). The reason Miss Gale included these short pieces in a collection of otherwise substantial essays is explained by the apparent validation the two books are intended to give to her own ideas; both of them treat man's so-called new awakening to his psychic possibilities. Courtney is alarmed by J. B. Watson's popular theories describing human behavior in terms of mere motor activities devoid of feelings and images. After attempting to discredit them, Courtney argues that a person's real "I" exists independent of his body. This other self, which Zona Gale called our allotrope, consists of an inner dimension ascertained not by introspection but by what Courtney insists upon calling "awareness." Introspection, he says, is merely a cerebral or motor operation normally used to know the outside world, but awareness can only be used within. Scientific determinism such as Watsonian psychology all but destroys this capacity for awareness. If it can be reinstated, he argues, it will save us from spiritual annihilation; Zona Gale in her review asserted it may again introduce us to "our old friend and complete stranger, 'I'." Slightly less enthusiastic about Courtney's promises of psychic resurrection, the *Saturday Review of Literature* drowsily called his whole effort "a pretentious little book," "a negligible playet [sic] of ideas."[9]

In extending Courtney's ideas even further, Saurat's volume excited Miss Gale into thinking it a book "of the utmost importance . . . the last word in the science of discovering the nature of being." His argument is that three conventions—material, moral, and metaphysical—will successively bring mankind into a perception of reality. Evidence that physical and moral laws already have documented the first two stages leads to speculation that the discovery of a body of ideas true for all minds will prove the validity of the final stage; they will, in fact, introduce mankind to such marvelous truths as to make anyone denying immortality, for example, impossibly blind.

In this whole collection of essays, plus the two reviews, Zona Gale's stratagem is essentially to "drop" her literary theory into the pebbly sky of metaphysics and hope to catch, with Thoreau, two fish on the same hook: accurate, down-to-earth realism and lofty spirituality. The tension between the two is ultimately to disappear in favor of the spirit which alchemically disembodies man by elevating him to the position of deity. In such a process, the human condition is annulled and the conflict between good and evil terminated. As in Whitman's "Passage to India," the "I" and the soul become one which "masterest the orbs," "matest Time," "smilest content at Death," and "fillest, swellest full the vastnesses of Space." The old drama of the soul suspended by a thread over hell loses all meaning. The terrors of sin and judgment, the tormented conscience, and the supplication for grace are likewise meaningless when the redeeming light comes merely by one's intuiting that his *real* self, after all, is not sinful but holy: not man-like but God-like.

Holding to this belief, the novelist would be guilty of heresy in depicting man as full of sin and woe, unless in later chapters he manipulates his unfortunate but not *dis-graced* protagonist into a higher consciousness informing him that what his fullness really consists of is not ugliness but beauty. If the artist chooses to confine all his characters to a lower plane of existence, then he risks the criticism of having himself a too-limited vision. Zona Gale attempted both reaches; her realistic fiction proves her success at one end and her essays in *Portage, Wisconsin* indicate her longing for success at the other.

IV

"There is no contemporary author whose evolution is more interesting than that of Zona Gale," wrote Joseph Wood Krutch after Alfred Knopf published *Borgia* in 1929.[10] Behind her now were novels ranging from syrup to vinegar to ambrosia, and criticism surveying the whole. Probably the key statement in all her critical theories came in the essay "Beauty and the Commonplace," in which she wrote: "The fiction of the future will realize angels in the commonplace." After such a prophecy, one would naturally await Zona Gale's next fictional work and expect therein to find a few angels. What the reader came to was *Borgia*, first serialized in *Scribner's*; what he found in it was Marfa Manchester, who, in truth, was a little lower than the angels. Nevertheless she was a strange woman and certainly not another Lulu Bett or Leda Perrin.

Krutch was certain he found something in the novel that "smells unpleasantly of New Thought and the Yogi of California." In this discovery he was correct. Enamoured more of her esoteric theories than of art, Miss Gale disastrously chose to expound metaphysics rather than to create convincing situations of metaphysical import. Making her intentions so ruinously explicit grew from her longing "to have people understand this book."[11] She admitted that the last third of the novel gave her trouble. Whatever her stumbling blocks, the book fails to match conception with performance and therefore falls short of art. Nevertheless, it underscores once again her intrepid concern with the invisible world and her identity in it.

The problem she poses concerns the nature of evil. Though

hardly of the magnitude of a whale hunt, the action centers upon Marfa, who is morbidly bewildered because she suspects she herself is an agent of evil. Everything she touches turns to disaster. A seemingly harmless young grocer's daughter of attractive proportions, Marfa innocently and completely involuntarily spreads her poison everywhere. Paul Barber went with Marfa to Stella's house where he caught diphtheria and later died. At Marfa's request Max Gavin promises to visit her, but on his way he collides with a truck and is left paralyzed for life. With a profligate husband and a shack full of miserable children, the cleaning lady's wretched life was likewise traceable to some light words Marfa once dropped. Marfa suggested the Dells as the spot for a family picnic, and little cousin Ben was drowned. Maud Brand was so jealous of Marfa that she died of a heart attack. Marfa's flirtations with Mr. Bartholomew led to a divorce with his wife. The squirrel Marfa intended to miss lay dead in the car's tracks.

By weaving all this evil mystery into commonplace happenings, Zona Gale intended something terribly esoteric. Echoing Marshall Pitt's puzzlement in *Birth,* Marfa wonders what to make of a world wherein even a chance word brings death and misery. Incredulous that such things could ever have happened to a Saint Francis, she thinks that perhaps something is wrong not with the universe but with her. (Donald Davidson perversely considered *this* thought the one "refreshing" aspect of the novel.)[12] Haunting Marfa are Max Gavin's words: "If you want the truth, you're probably all out of key." He said she needed to get her body "polarized to draw the good and not the ill." Marfa resolves, therefore, to re-make herself "so certain things'll follow me instead of the devilish ones."

Confused, like a primitive rising from Middle West ooze (Zona Gale's image), the twenty-three-year-old Marfa exclaims, "My God, *I'm* real." This is her turning point. Max was right: she had been an "inharmonious person." Now she confronts her real identity, not an evil Borgia but someone perhaps as perfect as "tree and star." With the mystic's gift, she sees beauty like a meteor-flash; suddenly she becomes "an island of being in a sea of non-being." And as long as she can continue to subdue flesh to spirit, she will be "right" with the world.

Being spiritually harmonious with all things is also the theme of Miss Gale's short story "Here! Here! Here!" which appeared in *Scribner's Magazine* four months before the Borgia serial started.[13] Lena in this story experiences the same subliminal consciousness when "like a bird alighting, one thought suddenly filled all her thought": spirit was with spirit.

One finds little in this fiction to satisfy an intellectual appetite. In his review Donald Davidson said he failed to discover anything that was more substantial than chewing gum. Zona Gale's attempts to describe the spiritually awakened individual rarely match her skill in depicting persons who are still spiritually asleep. Her metaphysical intentions smother her execution; her theories kill artistic performance.

As if to suggest that after mystical illumination one must again return to the light of common day, Zona Gale left her readers on the pinnacle of *Borgia* but for a moment before plunging them into the oppressive everyday actualities in *Bridal Pond* (1930). In a similar way she earlier had followed *Preface to a Life* with *Yellow Gentians and Blue*. In her new book Marfa Manchester's dizzy ecstacies are nowhere to be found. Instead *Bridal Pond* contains realistic slices of life, thirteen short tales in a minor key. Only seldom do mystical strains show through. When they do, as in "Jailbird" and "Springtime," the enfolding gloom appears only darker. In the majority of these stories Zona Gale journeys into the depthless realms of the mind to find not beauty but guilt, frustration, and madness.

The stories provide an excellent cross-section of her literary forte: the provocative and nimbly told short story. Reaching as far back as 1909 for her *Atlantic Monthly* piece, "The Cobweb," she carefully chose for this book her best uncollected short fiction. The result assuredly shows her as an adroit stylist whose eye and ear deftly catch the Portage moment.

Weakest among these stories are "The Cobweb" and "White Bread"; they are better than most of the small-town chronicles written during her Friendship Village period but still too thickly coated with cake icing. Other stories in the collection achieve a quivering intensity. Her tight style restrains poignant sympathies for the oppressed and inarticulate, for the sadly limited people who hope to no avail, who toil and die. The promise of America in "Springtime" fails to match the hardships suffered through a Chicago winter by an ignorant and destitute immigrant peasant family. "Tattie" recounts the pathetic loneliness of a middle-aged house servant to whose wedding no bridegroom comes. After a night-long but futile vigil, Tattie folds her wedding dress away and greets the dawn the only way she knows how: "I'll have to keep on. Seems like there's nothing else to do." "Wisconsin Note-Book" tells of the aging Rippletons, heartlessly crushed by big business. In "The Dime" the knowledge that his failing eyesight inconveniences his daughter's household finally breaks Grandfather Tarkoff's self-respect; and, like Grandfather Crumb in *Faint Perfume*, the useless man drowns himself in the river. His daughter recognizes that he had tied a long rope to a tree and fastened the other end to his leg " 'So's not to make us any [more] trouble, having him washed away.' "

Zona Gale's interest in abnormal minds and circumstances produced her best stories in *Bridal Pond*. In "Tobacco Shop" old Orlo Melt, the tobacconist, returned a blow to the face of a customer who, impatient with Melt's slowness, struck him. Thinking he has killed the customer, Melt flees. Before mustering nerve to return to the shop where in fact the customer had fallen dazed but not dead, Melt wildly roams the streets now changed into a terrifying labyrinth where in everyone's eye his imagined guilt is known.

More of this kind of nightmare comes in "Brendy," the story of a gardener who works among Miss Mardo's tulips while all the time desiring her. On her wedding night he helps the bride and groom escape the pursuing well-wishers by trading cars; into the night he madly drives their car covered with streamers and "Just Married" signs. The lingering fragrance of Miss Mardo . . . the laughter and horns . . . the thought of himself "tall and clean and rich" taking her "where the curtains were red and soft" . . . in short, the thought that "he was like any other man" and the knowledge that he was not overwhelmed him. His right foot bore down. In a crash which no one heard "Weldon's wood received him"; the darkness of the wood closed about him "in clean blackness, forever."

The story "Bridal Pond," from which the book takes its title, is Zona Gale's most successful effort to explore the regions of insanity. Jens Jevins, the richest farmer in the county, confesses before the court to the murder of his wife Agna. He said his plan had first been to shoot her, but he had decided later to push her into the pond close by his farm. Boys playing there the preceding night had interfered with this second plan, but he remembered, when there, that Agna, fancying that a car could easily miss the turn and hurtle into the pond, had shivered in the warm air. Unable to sleep that night, Jens told the court, he woke Agna and asked her to return to the pond where they arrived in time to see headlights bearing down on them. As the car pitched past and into the pond, Jens said he imagined seeing himself and Agna in that car as they were on their wedding night thirty-seven years ago, he in his new suit and she in her blue dress. It was as if he had "reached back into the past and killed her."

Unable to understand his story, the bewildered court members sit silent, then are suddenly interrupted by shouts outside that somebody has just pulled a car with wedding streamers out of Jevins' pond. Jens and the others run to see two silent "passionless" figures, in new suit and blue dress, dead. Startled by the commotion, Agna hurries down to the pond and tells one of the court members, who asked her if she and Jens had seen the car when they were out last night, that neither one had been outside during the night. Jens, who suddenly breaks loose screaming "Jens, Jens, Agna," throws himself beside the bodies. Now obviously demented, he insists to the horrified crowd that he and Agna had both died on their bridal night, "in the safety" of their youth.

In this allegory of death-in-life, Jens has awakened to the perception that for thirty-seven years of marriage he and Agna have been dead to a higher plane of existence and that his own lethargy killed her. This vision constitutes madness to both the crowd and, ironically, to his wife who has been blindly satisfied with "the slow rust of unending days." The story is dramatically unified and the language is unobtrusive and at times extraordinarily evocative ("The court-room was held as a ball of glass, in which black figures hang in arrested motion"). It leaves the reader with the tantalizing thought that Zona Gale's fiction, given more range and control, could have brought her into the front ranks of American literature.

CHAPTER 7

Final Years

I

ZONA GALE was fifty-four when she married William Llywelyn Breese, a Portage banker and stocking manufacturer whom she had known since childhood. Both had gone separately to Southern California in the spring of 1927 and, quite by accident, had met at Riverside where both were staying at Frank Miller's Mission Inn. Though Mr. Breese's first wife had died earlier leaving him with a daughter, Juliette, he had no intention of marrying again. But after he and Miss Gale returned to Portage, they renewed their acquaintance and were married in October, 1928. She moved into Breese's large, red-brick house which occupied the greater part of a block on MacFarlane Road. He had built it in 1912, and now for his new bride he greatly enlarged it by adding a richly carved, oak-paneled study, upstairs rooms, and a walled-in garden.

Her marriage marked an important milestone in her personal life, and in the same year *Portage, Wisconsin and Other Essays* summarized her preceding long years of fiction. She moved away from the Edgewater house where she and her parents had lived so intimately together and where now only her father remained. Furthermore, she and William Breese adopted a three-year-old girl named Leslyn to whose support Zona Gale had already contributed. Her abruptly new role was now that of wife and mother.

Even so, she wore no wedding ring, continued to sign her work "Zona Gale," and went about her business as before. She hired a governess to care for Leslyn and fourteen-year-old Juliette, and in the evenings she exchanged accounts with her husband about their separate day's activities. The transition with the past had been easily accomplished; she found she could be both Zona Gale and Mrs. Breese. With the death of her father on September 18, 1929, eleven months after her marriage, the transition crumbled; as Zona Gale, she found herself grief-stricken and alone. The death of her mother six years earlier had sent her wandering off into the spirit world and had, at the same time, resulted in her strangest fiction. After Zona Gale's earlier fiasco with Ridgely Torrence, her deeply personal affections had centered upon her parents, so that with her mother's death, and now her father's, something of inestimable importance ended.

After her father's death she turned over the old parental home to the Portage Women's Civic Club, and she renewed activities which frequently took her away from Portage. In 1930 she campaigned for Philip La Follette, who was running for the Wisconsin governorship once held by his inimitable father. During the winter of 1931 she joined the Open Forum Speakers' Bureau and lectured under its auspices on university campuses throughout the country. While at Rollins College in Winter Park, Florida, she received her fourth honorary doctoral degree, the three others having come from Ripon College (1922), University of Wisconsin (1929), and Mount Mary College in Milwaukee (1930). The next summer she covered the Republican National Convention in Chicago for the Milwaukee *Journal* and wrote two one-act plays, *The Clouds* and *Evening Clothes*. She declined a position as professor of journalism at Columbia University for the following autumn, but she took an active part during the summer of 1933 in Chicago's International Congress of Women to which she had been appointed as Wisconsin's representative. At this congress, whose theme was "Our Common Cause—Civilization," she united with such notables as Secretary of Labor Frances Perkins, Grace Abbott, Jane Addams, historian Mary R. Beard, and Mrs. Franklin D. Roosevelt in the common cause of international peace. In her spare time she collaborated with Marian deForest on twelve Friendship Village episodes for the National Broadcasting Company.

The two one-act plays added little to her literary stature. Both contained the usual ingredients of domestic realism more successfully blended in her fiction. In *The Clouds*, Misses Amy, Elsa, and Lily typically fritter away their emotions on trivia.

Final Years

In *Evening Clothes* the focus is sympathetically upon "Grandma" who learns that, because a "lot of borrowing" has been done without her knowledge, the Ebbit Mill is valueless and her last days will be spent in the poorhouse.

Of more consequence is the novelette, *Papa La Fleur,* which appeared early in 1933. As the story of a father and his two daughters unwinds to its melancholic end, one thinks of Zona Gale's own situation following her father's death. The theme of the story is that an old order gives way to a new, the two eras remaining forever separate. Papa La Fleur sells one of his two small river islands in order to finance Dolly's year in Chicago after her graduation. Now that her younger sister wants her chance, Papa La Fleur is driven to sell the second island, the only property he owns free and clear. Just why Linnie wants to go to Chicago, Papa La Fleur fails to understand, and his puzzlement is made more acute by the fact that Dolly never has told him since her return what had so changed her, silenced her, because of her year in the big city. The distance between the two generations cannot be bridged, and the island symbolizes Papa La Fleur's final payment or sacrifice to that which he cannot understand. "Abruptly he was alone in a world of which he knew nothing. That other world was gone, of the days when he had first planted the garden, built the house, bought the island." The language of his daughters' generation he does not understand, and his own language is too distant for them. In his final effort to reach the island, which represents for him all of the past that still remains, strange river currents catch his canoe and pull it under.

In marrying William Breese, Zona Gale's own departure from her father's home should not be interpreted as parallel with that of Papa La Fleur's daughters. The parallel is rather between herself and Papa La Fleur, for both recognize that something precious has passed away. For Papa La Fleur it was his island, his generation, his small but significant conquests—in short, his identity. For Zona Gale it was the trinity with her parents and the myriad associations surrounding her parental home. For both, the little place each made for himself was disappearing. A pang comes to Papa La Fleur each time his daughters insist they are "separate" persons, that their world is no longer his. Zona Gale felt the same way in seeing her idyllic world recede; her language about these things was unintelligible to her husband and daughters.

It was appropriate that her next volume was a collection of stories bearing the title, *Old Fashioned Tales,* published later the same year. The stories are undistinguished; most of them should never have been resurrected from the popular magazines where they had first appeared. But the more important fact is that they take the reader far back to this idyllic world— back to the time when Zona Gale's sentiments were colored so richly by the innocence with which she looked upon human relations. That this innocence was never lost accounts for the central feature in her whole fictional output: the coexistence of "sweet sentiment" and "bitter brew."[1] The bitterest brew of all was separation from her own lost island; it could be recovered only through memories and such stories as these which depict peace in a family-like village.

II

After the publication of *Papa La Fleur, Old Fashioned Tales,* and, in 1934, a one-act dramatic adaptation of her novel *Faint Perfume,* Zona Gale's literary career was practically over. She was still politically active and, in the mid-1930's, still keenly interested in Wisconsin education, especially at Madison. In 1923 Wisconsin's progressive Republican Governor John Blaine had appointed her regent of the University of Wisconsin, primarily because of her long-time effort to establish equal educational rights for women.[2] After her appointment she plunged into many other matters of university policy. When the regents refused in 1925 a proffered gift from the General Board of Education, she strongly supported their action which thenceforth prohibited the University from accepting any "gifts, donations, or subsidies . . . from any incorporated educational endowments or organizations of like character."[3] Her argument defending this action cited the danger of potential control by businessmen who, with their "tainted money," sought to endow the institution. The same year, as a member of the committee to appoint a successor to President E. A. Birge, Zona Gale was a leading influence in the selection of thirty-eight-year-old Glenn Frank, then editor of *Century Magazine.*

Little did she suspect the distress this appointment would cause her personally in later years. From the outset the so-called "boy president" was a stormy figure, and it was not until several months after his dismissal in 1936 that the tempest finally subsided. Two years before Governor Philip La Follette threw him out, the battle lines were clearly drawn, and Zona Gale was a chief spokesman in Frank's defense. The first dramatic exchange of blows came in Mencken's *American Mercury* where Ernest L. Meyer's searing criticism of President Frank summoned Zona Gale to arms in the subsequent issue.[4]

In his attack Meyer wrote: "It took the campus two years to doubt him, four to see through him, and six to regard him with amused contempt. And today, eight years after his arrival, he has probably not a single admirer left among the host who hailed his coming with hosannas." Illustrating Frank's failure as an administrator, Meyer cited the collapse, after only five years, of Dr. Alexander Meikeljohn's Experimental College which Frank had originally fostered. Meyer's real target, however, was Frank himself: his imperceptiveness to faculty sentiment; his prudery in forbidding Dora Russell, wife of philosopher Bertrand Russell, to speak on the campus after he learned her views on sex and women's rights in marriage; his condescension toward local citizens including faculty in favor of big Chicago businessmen; his superficial learning, clichés, pretentiousness, Billy Sunday oratory, and, most fatally, "the Methodism in his madness." Quoting President Frank as having said one year after his appointment, "'It is still a mystery to me why I was asked,'" Meyer added: "Today it is not Glenn Frank who puts the query, but the campus of the University of Wisconsin."

Zona Gale's reply beautifully illustrates the poise and kindly graciousness which characterize all her statements even on the most controversial subjects. In contrast with Meyer's vilifications, she merely described the four areas in which she thought Frank's record to be exemplary: revamping the curriculum to improve scholarship and increase independent study; inaugurating Dr. Meikeljohn's Experimental College to integrate subjects to be studied; establishing the Bureau of Guidance and Records to discourage unfit students from entering the University; and providing an atmosphere of liberalism to encourage the unhampered exchange of ideas.

Both spokesmen were silent on the central issue which H. L. Mencken noticed as early as 1927 when he predicted that President Frank would sometime be a good candidate for the White House.[5] Governor Philip La Follette and his brother, Senator Robert M. La Follette, Jr., who together held the reins of the Progressive party, surmised the same thing. When in January, 1936, Governor La Follette appointed five Progressives to fill vacancies in the University's board of regents, the rumor immediately spread that he was lining up votes to oust President Frank.[6] Because Philip La Follette himself loomed as a potential presidential candidate, national publicity emphasized the Frank–La Follette political issue rather than questions about Frank's competence as a university president.

Zona Gale now found herself in the distressing position of having to choose sides in this new alignment. For thirty years she had worked for the La Follette cause. "The La Follette name," she wrote in 1928, "stands for a sovereign service: namely, the socialization of a State, and of more than a State."[7] This same year she also defended Frank in the Dora Russell incident; and she heard him magniloquently tell her the next year, when conferring the honorary Doctor of Letters degree upon her, that she had given Wisconsin "her place in the sun of letters"!

She found it hard to believe not only that Philip La Follette would issue the order that Glenn Frank had to go but that, as it was rumored, certain regents were called to the governor's office and given the same ultimatum. Among the Zona Gale papers is a stray note, addressed to no one and written in pencil, stating that in her opinion outside influence coming from the governor against the president was "not the progressive way." She found it incredible that a La Follette would "go about a thing that way."

Whether justice was or was not done becomes a moot question when political considerations steal into the picture. The *Nation* saw no cause for criticizing La Follette's action against Frank; two men, both eyeing the White House, "just don't love each other. . . . That's it."[8] *News-Week*, not hiding its bias either, implied that Frank was the victim of shady partisan politics. Its account quoted Zona Gale as having said he was "a ray of good influence," and it then cited regent Clara T. Runge's explanation for his dismissal: "He has not been such a good

Progressive."⁹ To Zona Gale, personally involved on both sides, the "Glenn Frank mistake" was not his but La Follette's—"so stupid, so incredible."¹⁰

Her break with La Follette was soon in the open. She requested the Civil Liberties Committee and the American Association of University Professors to investigate; she tried to influence regents, columnists, and organizations to her side. But all her efforts on behalf of Frank failed, and by the spring of 1937 the furor was over. Tired and discouraged, saddened by her quarrel with La Follette whose name had been inviolable for her through the years, she wanted to get away, and far away, from what had become a transformed Wisconsin. Invitations to visit Japan from Yone Naguchi and other Japanese friends whom she had first met at Frank Miller's Mission Inn were too tempting to resist any longer.

III

Simultaneous to Zona's departure for Japan appeared her novel *Light Woman*, her last book of fiction published before her death. It failed to arouse much attention. E. H. Walton in the New York *Times* (April 4, 1937) marked it off as a "perfunctory little book which Miss Gale's admirers would do well to forget about quickly." The highest praise it received came from reviewers who thought it should be adapted as good comedy for the stage. *Light Woman* can hardly be called great, or even good, without qualifying one's definition. The characters resemble puppets, their motivations are barely explored or developed. But for what the novel reveals about the author—at this time of her ominously growing perplexity about the dichotomies of past and future, youth and age, peace and anxiety— *Light Woman* becomes biographically if not artistically important.

This novel extends the theme seen in *Papa La Fleur* and again touches her own new role as Mrs. Breese, separated from her deceased parents, their home, and their simple pieties. Mitty, the "light woman" of the title, is a modern young girl who wishes for nothing more than some fun—despite the consequences she is too shallow to perceive. Her plan is to pose as Nicholas Belden's wife and then to accompany him home to his father's farm. "They will ne-ver know the difference," Mitty jokes. "They will think we are married in the same holy bonds which bind—and gag—all of them." Despite his uneasiness, Nicholas refrains from interfering in his lover's plan.

Of course, old Matthew Belden, the father, believes her story; and, to Mitty's heightened amusement, the neighbors believe it too. When Nicholas warns her that the people are planning a charivari for them, she delightfully laughs: "Cat-Cat [Cataraugus] County is a terribly serious place, isn't it, Nicky." Inadvertently, Mitty blurts out—when alone with Ratcliff, who is courting Anne Belden—that she is not married; and, during a later quarrel between old Matthew and Ratcliff, Mitty's secret comes out. Dumbfounded, old Matthew cannot understand how anyone could take his old-fashioned credulity so lightly. There was for him "no bridge across this narrow chasm of the generations, too wide for words to span." To him, Mitty's furious little speech rings hollow: "You're all so sure, so sure of marriage, so sure of rules, rules, rules! So sure that whatever one wants to do is wrong! And where has it got us? Is your world so fine—is it? That old world—I do not call it orderly. But there is a new world and I live in that world. I hate your rules! I do what I think!"

Coming in Zona Gale's earlier fiction, Mitty's speech would have perfectly expressed one of her major themes: freedom from conventions. One wishes Lulu Bett had had the gumption to utter it. The new and unforeseeable fact about Mitty, who has declared her independence, is that respect for the past has become contempt. Callousness has replaced deference. "Holy bonds" of marriage are nothing more than a "gag." The past with all its idealism is taken lightly, laughingly, contemptuously by Mitty and her new generation. Once Zona Gale uttered speeches like Mitty's; once she looked forward to a new world freed from the stifling conventions of the old. Now, two years before death, she fears what rebellion brings and longs for yesterday's Golden Age and its Friendship Villagers.

Her trip to Japan was the antidote she needed after her exhausting involvement in the Glenn Frank affair. Furthermore, it came at a time when she felt herself ever more adrift and alone and beyond any solace her husband and daughters could provide. Going to Japan was to find the well-spring—or what old Matthew Belden in *Light Woman* called the "center of old energy"—from which her own life had found its deepest nourishment. Oriental mystery and mysticism offered the spiritual comfort lacking in the square and solid red-brick house on MacFarlane Road where, to her, an unknown Mrs. Breese lived.

The weeks she spent in Japan were full of the usual fare: receptions, lectures to university students, official introductions to both Japanese and American dignitaries, speeches urging inseparable friendship between the two nations, and closely scheduled tours. She enjoyed all these affairs, but far more fructifying were her leisurely drives into the countryside to see the little villages, the gabled and tiled roofs, the azaleas and moss and waterfalls and lanterns. "It is all here," she exclaimed to Pearl Buck.[11] "All is now a window where once had been a wall."[12]

She returned in late autumn eager to write a book about her trip and also to begin what she called "the inevitable" autobiographical work. But her stopover at Mission Inn again had quickened her interest in Wisconsin-born Frank Miller, whose death in 1935 was the occasion for her writing a long commemorative article published the same year in *Christian Century*.[13] Her decision now to write Miller's biography ironically prevented the completion of her own, for six months after *Frank Miller of Mission Inn* appeared, Zona Gale was dead.

Her 1927 visit to Miller's celebrated inn impressed her not only because of the inn's enchanting decor but also because of the philosophy Miller sought to express through it. Heavily underwritten by Henry Huntington, the place was first intended as a hotel; but through Miller's effort, it later grew into a shrine to California's Hispanic past. Miller, however, intended something more; he wanted to provide a spiritual oasis where, through the ministration of beauty, guests could find the meaning in his motto: "The world's greatest need is a sense of the intangible."[14]

With its high bell-towers, arched cloisters, and spacious central patio, the inn closely resembled California's old Spanish missions. And when strolling amid its bougainvillea, orange trees, and palms, guests could easily imagine themselves in an old mission garden. Inside the inn were rooms exquisitely furnished with imported *objets* which Frank Miller and his wife Marion had collected from many parts of the world. Like an old baronial hall in a Spanish castle, the inn's long music room was magnificently impressive. Its floors of oak

squares, its wooden beams, carved gilt lamps, sconces, cande-
labra, banners, rare old chairs, a collection of over three hundred
Christian crosses—everything served to express Miller's belief
that beauty with quietness necessarily accompanied hospitality,
itself a noble thing. All these furnishings, this atmosphere, immensely appealed to Zona Gale who looked upon Frank Miller,
the innkeeper, as an "intuitionist," "to-morrow's man," one "at
home in his universe."

To the last, Zona Gale believed that universal love was an art
man would master. Clues to its approach she found, abstractly,
in such a man as Frank Miller whose feeling for the intangible
supposedly lifted him above the petty animosities which comprise
all too much of daily living. At Mission Inn rather than on
MacFarlane Road in Portage she found the kind of "love force"
which she believed would inevitably weld all nations together.
This same force was the "religion" preached by another such
man, Alexander, Duke of Russia, who came to the United States
in 1930 as an exile from the Bolshevist Revolution. Zona Gale
thought that he too showed a profound understanding of love.
In his books *Religion of Love* (1929), *Spiritual Education* (1930),
and *Union of Souls* (1931) she recognized a kindred writer whose
belief that man not only has a soul but *is* one, underscored her
own life-long conviction that man is "something more."

Undoubtedly this lofty idealism, in the abstract, would have
constituted large parts of the autobiography she wished to write
but never completed. Before illness forced her to discontinue it
after the first chapter, she arranged for the publication of *Magna*
(posthumously published in 1939) which in December to February of 1932-1933 had appeared serially in *Harper's Magazine*.
Love was its theme, the same kind of idealistic love Frank Miller,
Alexander, Yone Naguchi, and Tagore platonically professed.
Written prior to *Papa La Fleur* and *Light Woman*, it affirms
love's mystic potency which to old La Fleur, Matthew Belden,
and the novelist herself in 1938, seemed absent in the new
generation.

The novelette is in fact a study in the "levels" of love: from
Earl Pethner to Bolo Marks who respectively murder and marry
their lovers. Earl's love for Helga is madness; Alec's love for
Magna is physical ecstasy—or rather it is potentially so, as much
as a midnight kiss in a Zona Gale novel can arouse. But in Bolo's

love for Magna there is neither madness nor emotional storm
but rather "the warmth and peace of the sun." This was love as
spiritual union. If a still higher love exists, clues come from
old Lydia who intermittently appears in the story to announce
that her husband, Jute, who for twenty years has been in his
grave, "is coming home to-night." This is love death cannot touch.
    Again in *Magna* Zona Gale characteristically fastens weighty
ideas to thin straws. One's reluctance in assenting to these ideas
is due to suspicion that the world of mind and spirit is too
complex to be audaciously summarized, for instance, by old
Lydia. By not complicating her ideas, Zona Gale hopes that a
spoken line or image will carry the burden of their complexity.
Poetry succeeds in this compression. Something electric, a fine
frenzy, can be compounded from imagination and the precise
statement. In such a way Zona Gale intended her slender novel
to envelop realms of abstractions about love. However, she did
not completely avoid the danger of having this compression
lead only to cracked wisdom.
    As a delicate portrayal of Magna's first love and then of her
tranquil acquiescence to more mature love requiring neither
moonlight nor music to sustain it, this novel is as sophisticated as
anything Zona Gale wrote. A similar polish gives works like *Miss
Lulu Bett, Faint Perfume,* parts of *Birth,* and certain stories in
Bridal Pond their verisimilitude. But Zona Gale expected more
from *Magna* and from such novels as *Preface to a Life* and
Borgia. Her predilection for ideas about the intangible in *Magna*
too often befogged the clean, hard lines of her realism. Thinking
her delicate and often successful art insufficient to stand by
itself, she hung huge, evanescent conceptualizations upon it, as
if she hoped to fortify already good wine with wood spirit.
    Her death from pneumonia came fast. Ridgely Torrence's
Christmas letter sent to encourage her recovery arrived on the
day she died, December 27, 1938. Three days later she was
buried in the Silver Lake cemetery outside Portage. Despite the
sub-zero weather, the Presbyterian Church was filled to over-
flowing with dignitaries from the state and with local residents,
mostly middle-aged or elderly. Outside the church door stood
three Winnebago women whom Zona Gale had frequently be-
friended. After Glenn Frank spoke a few words, Dr. Ralph B.
Hyman of Buffalo, who conducted the service, closed with Zona

Gale's own words: "'The world is just beginning—I must go now and serve the king.'" The cortege then slowly wound its way over the iron ground blanketed with snow.

IV

Reading through the three-foot bookshelf of Zona Gale's works reminds one of Washington Irving's melancholic reflections when he stood before the dusty shelves in the Westminister Abbey library.

> How much, thought I, has each of these volumes, now thrust aside with such indifference, cost some aching head! how many weary days! how many sleepless nights! . . . And all for what? to occupy an inch of dusty shelf—to have the title of their works read now and then in a future age, by some drowsy churchman or casual straggler like myself; and in another age to be lost, even to remembrance. Such is the amount of this boasted immortality. A mere temporary rumor, a local sound; like the tone of that bell which has just tolled among these towers, filling the ear for a moment—lingering transiently in echo—and then passing away like a thing that was not ("The Mutability of Literature" from *The Sketch Book*).

One is safe in saying that few persons in recent years have read many Zona Gale novels. Some may remember *Miss Lulu Bett*; others her magazine articles on women's rights or La Follette Progressivism. Among younger readers whose memories only dimly touch the stock market crash of 1929, the Lindberg kidnapping case, the National Recovery Act, or the Spanish Civil War, Zona Gale's books may have no significance whatsoever. Generally disregarded and now out of print, they invite little interest except to an occasional literary historian or to a "casual straggler."

To someone rediscovering them or to the person coming to them for his first time, their effect strangely echoes Walt Whitman's prophecy that who touches *Leaves of Grass* "touches a man." From these Wisconsin books more than a novelist, a reformer, or a Portage citizen emerges; for whoever comes to them comes to Zona Gale, the woman. Though anyone reading her work might find it vulnerable to criticism in matters of

technique and subject matter, Zona Gale's solid core, her private
character, remains unscathed. The reader recognizes a woman
far too well-informed and articulate to remain silent, yet too
modest to seek the limelight: a woman whose words may have
been many-edged but never deceitful. What she wrote, she un-
ashamedly believed. If she wavered, her doubts were noble ones.

At first glance her world of Portage is too remote today
for serious concern, for all about are the more urgent issues of
world revolutions, rockets to outer space, genocidal weapons,
and Johnny's chance for college. To the hurrying American
pursuing what he can seldom define, Zona Gale's relevance is
indeed tenuous. Perhaps her fictional Dwight Deacon and Orrin
Crumb, like Sinclair Lewis' Babbitt, still reflect American ambi-
tion in business; but, after all, this subject has run its course and
is now stale beer. Furthermore, her rebellion against Victorian
prudery has won its victory—thanks to the less than flamboyant
efforts of women like Zona Gale. Her efforts in behalf of women
suffrage were long ago successful, and the domestic treadmill
which she saw blighting American womanhood has now become
Gracious Living. The small towns like Portage are no longer
isolated; television brings a Chicago ball-game or a variety show
to any family sufficiently solvent to afford a five-dollar down-
payment. If further evidence is needed to show her distance
from today's reader, the fact that she died believing Neville
Chamberlain had averted war with Hitler should suffice.

Zona Gale's case, however, is not so simply closed. Underneath
her social criticism and domestic satire was the conviction that
people have dignity which no individual, business, or government has the right to exploit. In her early Friendship Village
stories this dignity lacked the sinew necessary to save it from
sentimentality. In attempting to depict the inherent value in
simple people, she was overly naïve. But she widened her dimensions of observation to show these people heroically fighting to
stave off doubts about their own human value. Suddenly the
reader confronts the contemporaneity of her theme; it is of the
little man in a world he never made.

As for social and political thinking, her reformist activities
forty years ago, like those of Jane Addams, would put her in the
vanguard even today. Her advocacy of liberal legislation rested
on the assumption—still far from universally accepted—that

equality of human dignity logically leads to equality of opportunity. In a country where national issues find too few feminine leaders, Zona Gale's example is worth imitating. In her day she took the side of the immigrant, the employee, the child-laborer, and the helpless underdog ruthlessly exploited by business and government alike. She joined with those whose intelligence and courage led to reform. She thought principles of human dignity to be more important than capital gains, an attitude which she would discover still unpopular today among many.

An even more crucial consideration about Zona Gale revolves around her open use of such words as *peace, love, cooperation, sacrifice.* These words could catapult her back into a Tennysonian dream or they could whisk her into urgent contemporaneity. Hemingway called such words obscene, unsuited for this century. Persons using them were "talking a lot of rot" because, instead of wanting peace-love-cooperation-sacrifice, these same people thrived and grew rich on war-hate-competition and someone else's sacrifice. One's whole era, Hemingway implied in *Farewell to Arms,* so blatantly misrepresents these ideals that to voice them is to be either an obscene fool or an uninitiated child.

Neither a fool nor a child, Zona Gale frequently voiced them, sentimentally at first but later resonantly as from an enriched and intensified conviction. The reader may challenge the assumptions upon which they rest; he may question the logic used to structure them and the sufficiency of experience necessary to test them. Yet despite all efforts to demolish them, they still may remain inexplicably valid. All that remains for the unconvinced reader to do is to grow weary of them, as Melville did of Emerson's intransigent faith in man's goodness. This same weariness comes to one reading Zona Gale's assurances about man's capacity to achieve peace and universal love. But to decry her ideals as being out of joint with the times is not to invalidate them. Nor is voicing them necessarily obscene— when one remembers Hawthorne's warning to the old New Englanders that, because they did not talk about their ideals, they might someday cease to feel about them. Because Zona Gale often failed to dramatize these ideals compellingly does not mean, therefore, that they are valueless or that they cost her no secret agony.

More to the point in a critical assessment is to judge the

artistic expression of her ideas. Regardless of an artist's illusions, she is still responsible for unifying them with the reality of experience and then transforming them into some form of expression in which, in Eliot's terms, the dancer and the dance become one. All parts must unite into a single organism, yet each part should manifest its own complexity. Artistic success rests upon this paradox of integration and tension. In the case of Zona Gale, several parts of her fiction, when considered separately, show remarkable merit. Her conception, faithful observation, and language point to artistic achievement of a potentially high order. But her failure to sustain artistically the complexities of both illusion and reality leaves her considerably short of first-rate success. Needless to say, her failing is a common one. It comes not because the artist is unable to resolve his own ambivalences (Zona Gale's wavering between the mundane and the spiritual persisted to her death) but because the artist lacks the imagination to create a world in which these ambivalences powerfully interact.

The purpose of this study has not been to argue that Zona Gale is anything more than a minor figure or that she has been undeservedly "neglected." Her career amply proves the truism that a writer's reputation may have no connection with the quantity or quality of his work. Yet in her own way, Zona Gale will be remembered as a village laureate whose stories range from the saccharine to the bitter, from the idyllic to the mordantly critical. Her assemblage of village people—the spiritually awakened, the drudge, the deranged, the pathetic, the inarticulate, the kind-hearted—will continue to preserve for remembrance the American small town which, in national literature, has unfolded so much of national drama.

Notes and References

Chapter One

1. "Portage, Wisconsin," in *Portage, Wisconsin and Other Essays* (New York, 1929), p. 5.
2. Zona Gale to Hamlin Garland (March 17, 1921).
3. Hamlin Garland, *Afternoon Neighbors* (New York, 1934), p. 6.
4. Willa Cather to Zona Gale (Oct. 23, 1928).
5. Frederick J. Hoffman, *The Twenties: American Writing in the Postwar Decade* (New York, 1955), p. 328.
6. Carl Van Doren, *The American Novel 1789-1939* (New York, 1940), p. 298.
7. "'Father,'" in *Portage, Wisconsin and Other Essays*, pp. 59-60.
8. Zona Gale and Charles F. Gale to "Dear Friends" (August, 1923).
9. Quoted by Keene Sumner, "The Everlasting Persistence of This Western Girl," *The American Magazine*, XCI (June, 1921), 139.
10. Unpublished notes in Zona Gale Papers (State Historical Society of Wisconsin, hereinafter referred to as SHSW).
11. August Derleth, *Still Small Voice: The Biography of Zona Gale* (New York, 1940), pp. 10-11.
12. "On Being 'Superior,'" *The World Tomorrow*, IX (April, 1926), 118.
13. Edna Ferber, *A Peculiar Treasure* (New York, 1939), p. 145.
14. *Ibid.*, p. 145.
15. *The Bookman*, LVII (April, 1923), 168.
16. *Ibid.*, p. 168.
17. Zona Gale Papers (SHSW).
18. Charles Hanson Towne, *Adventures in Editing* (New York, 1926), pp. 130-33.
19. All cited letters to Torrence are in Ridgely Torrence Papers (Princeton University Library).

Chapter Two

1. Edmund Clarence Stedman to Zona Gale (Dec. 12, 1906).
2. Quoted by Holbrook Jackson, *The Eighteen Nineties: A Review of Art and Ideas at the Close of the Nineteenth Century* (London, 1913), p. 137.

3. Edmund Clarence Stedman to Zona Gale (Dec. 12, 1906).

4. Quoted by Sumner, *op. cit.*

5. *Ibid.*, p. 141.

6. Ruth Suckow, "The Folk Idea in American Life," *Scribner's Magazine*, LXXXVIII (September, 1930), 245-55.

7. "Implications," *The Yale Review*, XVIII (Autumn, 1928), 87.

8. *The Bookman*, LVII (April, 1923), 168.

9. Fannie Hurst, "Zona Gale," *The Bookman*, LIII (April, 1921), 123.

10. Frederick Tabor Cooper, "Friendship Village Love Stories," *The Bookman*, XXXI (March, 1910), 79.

11. Constance Rourke, "Transitions," *New Republic*, XXIII (Aug. 11, 1920), 315-16.

12. Towne, *Adventures in Editing*, p. 133.

13. Quoted by Robert Gard, *Grassroots Theater: A Search for Regional Arts in America* (University of Wisconsin Press, 1955), p. 88.

14. Quoted by A. M. Drummond, "A Countryside Theatre Experiment," *Quarterly Journal of Speech Education*, VI (February, 1920), 46-47.

15. *The Bookman*, LVII (April, 1923), 168.

16. Ellery Sedgwick to Zona Gale (Sept. 7, 1915).

17. Gilman Hall to Zona Gale (March 23, 1915).

18. Eliza Beers to Zona Gale (Dec. 3, 1915).

20. Gilman Hall to Zona Gale (March 23, 1915).

Chapter Three

1. Edward A. Fitzpatrick, *McCarthy of Wisconsin* (Columbia University Press, 1944), pp. 103-5.

2. Zona Gale to Robert M. La Follette, Jr. (n.d.).

3. "What the Day's Work Means to Me," *The Bookman*, XLII (November, 1915), 316.

4. Zone Gale to Walter Rauschenbusch (April 21, 1918).

5. "Sophisticate," *Christian Century*, LIV (March 3, 1937), 281.

6. "Frances Willard," *Christian Century*, LV (Jan. 26, 1938), 114.

7. Walter B. Rideout, *The Radical Novel in the United States 1900-1954* (Harvard University Press, 1956), p. 132.

8. Zona Gale to Sidney Howard (April 24, 1924).

9. Zona Gale to Speaker, State Senate, Pierre, South Dakota (Feb. 5, 1927).

10. Elmer Rice to Zona Gale (Feb. 3, 1931).

11. Mark Schorer to Harold P. Simonson (Sept. 12, 1960).

12. Baltimore *American* (Oct. 20, 1915); Chicago *Tribune* (Oct.

Notes and References

30, 1915); Chicago *Post* (Oct. 29, 1915); New York *Globe* (Dec. 4, 1915); Los Angeles *Express* (Nov. 10, 1915).

13. Jane Addams to Zona Gale (Aug. 3, 1915).

14. Mary Austin, "American Women and the Intellectual Life," *The Bookman*, LIII (August, 1921), 483.

15. "The Idle Forties," *Survey*, LVII (Dec. 1, 1926), 306.

16. "The Great Ladies of Chicago," *Survey*, LXVII (Feb. 1, 1932), 479.

17. "An Address: The Status of Wisconsin Women Under the Equal Rights Law" in *Proceedings of the State Bar Association of Wisconsin* (Madison, 1923), p. 185.

18. "Why I Shall Vote for La Follette," *New Republic*, XL (Oct. 1, 1924), 115.

19. Quoted by Russel B. Nye, *Midwestern Progressive Politics* (Michigan State College Press, 1951), p. 1.

20. *Ibid.*, p. 44.

21. *Ibid.*, p. 159.

22. Belle Case La Follette and Fola La Follette, *Robert M. La Follette* (New York, 1953), Vol. II, ch. xliii.

23. *Ibid.*, II, 778.

24. *Ibid.*, II, 792.

25. Porter Emerson Browne, "The Vigilantes, Who and Why and What They Are," *Outlook*, LXIX (May 8, 1918), 67-69.

26. "Correspondence Drafting La Follette," *Nation*, CXIX (July 23, 1924), 96.

Chapter Four

1. *The Bookman*, LVII (April, 1923), 170.

2. Arthur Hobson Quinn, *American Fiction: An Historical and Critical Survey* (New York, 1936), p. 702.

3. William Allen White, "Fiction of the Eighties and Nineties," in John Macy, ed., *American Writers on American Literature* (New York, 1931), p. 390.

4. Régis Michaud, *The American Novel To-day* (Boston, 1928), p. 249.

5. *The Bookman, loc. cit.*, p. 170.

6. Zona Gale to Mr. Krumbine (Oct. 24, 1925).

7. Zona Gale to Editor, *Century Magazine* (March 22, 1919).

8. Carl Van Doren, *Contemporary American Novelists 1900-1920* (New York, 1928), pp. 165-66.

9. Constance Rourke, "Transitions," *New Republic*, XXIII (Aug. 11, 1920), 316.

10. Fannie Hurst to Zona Gale (n.d.).

11. Edith Wharton to Zona Gale (Sept. 26, 1922).

12. Zona Gale to Edith Wharton (Oct. 4, 1922).

13. Zona Gale to Edith Wharton (Oct. 19, 1922).

14. Robert Benchley in his Foreword to Zona Gale's *Miss Lulu Bett, An American Comedy of Manners* (New York, 1929), p. xiv.

15. Sumner, *op. cit.*, p. 140.

16. Ludwig Lewisohn, "Native Plays," *Nation*, CXII (Feb. 2, 1921), 189.

17. *Ibid.*, p. 189.

18. Louis Untermeyer, *Heavens* (New York, 1922), p. 73.

19. Hamlin Garland, *My Friendly Contemporaries* (New York, 1932), p. 329.

20. Merle Curti, *The Growth of American Thought* (New York, 1951), ch. xx.

21. Carl Van Doren to Zona Gale (Dec. 28, 1922).

22. Edith Wharton to Zona Gale (April 14, 1923); Zona Gale to Edith Wharton (May 7, 1923).

Chapter Five

1. Zona Gale to Henry Chester Tracy (May 5, 1927).

2. Quoted by Hoffman, *op. cit.*, p. 282.

3. Mary Baker Eddy, *Science and Health with Key to the Scriptures* (Boston, n.d.), p. 468.

4. Sir Oliver Lodge, "The Latest Ideas in Physics," *Harper's Magazine*, CXLVIII (April, 1924), 662.

5. Hoffman, *op. cit.*, p. 291.

6. Review, "Beyond Behaviorism," in *Portage, Wisconsin and Other Essays* (New York, 1928), p. 203.

7. Theodore Dreiser, *Dawn* (New York, 1931), p. 522.

8. *The Diary and Sundry Observations of Thomas Alva Edison*, ed., Dagobert D. Runes (New York, 1948), p. 239.

9. Zona Gale to Dorothy Canfield Fisher (Feb. 2, 1927).

10. Unpublished notes, Zona Gale Papers (SHSW).

11. Zona Gale to Laura Chase (April 26, 1926).

12. *Portage, Wisconsin and Other Essays*, p. 19.

13. Zona Gale to Alice Bailey (Aug. 3, 1926).

14. Quoted by Hoffman, *op. cit.*, p. 253.

15. Zona Gale to Alice Bailey (Aug. 3, 1926).

16. H. L. Mencken to Zona Gale (n.d.).

17. New York *Sun* (Nov. 13, 1926); New York *Times Book Review* (Nov. 7, 1926).

18. Hoffman, *op. cit.*, p. 334.

19. W. J. Blyton, "Idealism in Recent Fiction," *The Hibbert Journal*, XXX (January, 1933), 236.
20. Upton Sinclair, *American Outpost* (New York, 1932), p. 45.
21. Helen Dreiser, *My Life with Dreiser* (New York, 1951), p. 216.
22. Zona Gale to Norman Thomas (May 18, 1926).
23. *Time*, XVI (Sept. 15, 1930), 33-34.

Chapter Six

1. Edith Wharton, "The Great American Novel," *Yale Review*, XVI (July, 1927), 646-56.
2. "Out of Nothing Into Somewhere," *The English Journal* (March, 1924), p. 177.
3. "National Epics of the Border," *Yale Review*, XI (July, 1922), 852-56.
4. Earl H. Rovit, "American Literature and 'The American Experience,'" *American Quarterly*, XIII (Summer, 1961), 119n.
5. Zona Gale to Helen Bridgman (May 22, 1927).
6. Zona Gale to Laura Wurtzel (April 26, 1924).
7. Wallace Fowlie, *Mallarmé* (University of Chicago Press, 1953), p. 264.
8. See Edmund Wilson, *Axel's Castle* (New York, 1931), p. 13.
9. *Saturday Review of Literature*, IV (Aug. 27, 1927), 78.
10. Joseph Wood Krutch, "Zona Gale's New Manner," *Nation*, CXXIX (Dec. 11, 1929), 725.
11. Zona Gale to Grant Overton (Jan. 8, 1930).
12. Donald Davidson, "A Worker of Ill," *Saturday Review of Literature*, VI (Nov. 23, 1929), 440.
13. "Here! Here! Here!" *Scribner's Magazine*, LXXXIII (March, 1928), 281-90.

Chapter Seven

1. *Books* (Oct. 15, 1933), p. 16.
2. "What of Coeducation?," *Atlantic Monthly*, CXIV (July, 1914), 95-106.
3. "Shall State Universities Take 'Tainted Money'?" *Nation*, CXXI (Sept. 20, 1925), 349-50.
4. Ernest L. Meyer, "Glenn Frank: Journalist on Parole," *American Mercury*, XXXI (February, 1934), 149-59; Zona Gale, "Some Achievements of Glenn Frank," *American Mercury*, XXXI (March, 1934), 381-83.
5. *American Mercury*, XI (June, 1927), 159.
6. *News-Week*, VII (March 21, 1936), 32-33.

7. "Americans We Like: The La Follette Family," *Nation,* CXXVI (Feb. 15, 1928), 180.

8. *Nation,* CXLIII (Dec. 26, 1936), 748.

9. *News-Week,* IX (Jan. 16, 1937), 16.

10. Zona Gale to Mrs. William Hard (March 30, 1937).

11. Zona Gale to Pearl Buck (June, 1937).

12. Zona Gale to Yone Naguchi (June 28, 1937).

13. "Master of the Inn," *Christian Century,* LII (Oct. 23, 1935), 1346-47.

14. *Frank Miller of Mission Inn* (New York, 1938), pp. 83-84.

Selected Bibliography

Because Zona Gale's entire works are too numerous to include in a selective bibliography, the reader should consult *The Reader's Guide to Periodical Literature* for lists of over 280 published stories, articles, and poems by Miss Gale. A separate list of nearly 150 stories included in anthologies and in volumes listed in Section I below can be found by consulting the *Short Story Index* (1953). The two largest repositories of primary material are the Ridgely Torrence Collection in the Princeton University Library and the Zona Gale Papers at the State Historical Society of Wisconsin, Madison.

PRIMARY SOURCES

1. Fiction

Romance Island (Indianapolis: Bobbs-Merrill Company, 1906).
The Loves of Pelleas and Etarre (New York: The Macmillan Company, 1907).
Friendship Village (New York: The Macmillan Company, 1908).
Friendship Village Love Stories (New York: The Macmillan Company, 1909).
Mothers to Men (New York: The Macmillan Company, 1911).
Christmas (New York: The Macmillan Company, 1912).
When I Was a Little Girl (New York: The Macmillan Company, 1913).
Neighborhood Stories (New York: The Macmillan Company, 1914).
Heart's Kindred (New York: The Macmillan Company, 1915).
A Daughter of the Morning (Indianapolis: Bobbs-Merrill Company, 1917).
Birth (New York: The Macmillan Company, 1918).
Peace in Friendship Village (New York: The Macmillan Company, 1919).
Miss Lulu Bett (New York: D. Appleton & Company, 1920).
Faint Perfume (New York: D. Appleton & Company, 1923).
Preface to a Life (New York: D. Appleton & Company, 1926).
Yellow Gentians and Blue (New York: D. Appleton & Company, 1927).
Borgia (New York: Alfred A. Knopf, Inc., 1929).

Bridal Pond (New York: Alfred A. Knopf, 1930).
Papa La Fleur (New York: D. Appleton & Company, 1933).
Old Fashioned Tales (New York: Appleton-Century Company, Inc., 1933).
Light Woman (New York: Appleton-Century Company, Inc., 1937).
Magna (New York: Appleton-Century, Inc., 1939).

2. Non-Fiction

Civic Improvement in the Little Towns (Washington, D.C., American Civic Association, 1913).
What Women Won In Wisconsin (Washington, D.C., National Woman's Party, 1922).
Portage, Wisconsin and Other Essays (New York: Alfred A. Knopf, 1928).
Frank Miller of Mission Inn (New York: Appleton-Century Company, Inc., 1938).

3. Poetry

The Secret Way (New York: The Macmillan Company, 1921).

4. Drama

The Neighbors, in T. H. Dickinson, ed., *Wisconsin Plays* (New York: B. W. Huebsch, 1914).
Miss Lulu Bett (New York: D. Appleton & Company, 1921).
Uncle Jimmy (Boston: Walter H. Baker Company, 1922).
Mister Pitt (New York: D. Appleton & Company, 1925).
The Clouds (New York: Samuel French, Inc., 1932).
Evening Clothes (Boston: Walter H. Baker Company, 1932).
Faint Perfume (New York: Samuel French, Inc., 1934).

SECONDARY SOURCES

COOPER, FREDERICK TABOR. "Friendship Village Love Stories," *The Bookman*, XXXI (March, 1910), 79. Useful introduction to Zona Gale's early style and subject matter.
DAVIDSON, DONALD. "A Worker of Ill," *The Saturday Review of Literature*, VI (Nov. 23, 1929), 440. Review of *Borgia* and discussion of Zona Gale's broader work.
DERLETH, AUGUST. *Still Small Voice: The Biography of Zona Gale* (New York, 1940). The only previous full-length biography;

more anecdotal than critical. Contains first chapter of Zona Gale's unfinished autobiography.

Dictionary of American Biography, 2nd supplement (New York, 1958).

FERBER, EDNA. *A Peculiar Treasure* (New York, 1939). An autobiography with brief reference to Zona Gale as a Milwaukee newspaperwoman.

FITZPATRICK, EDWARD A. *McCarthy of Wisconsin* (New York, 1944). An account of Charles McCarthy's activities in the Wisconsin legislature, with references to Zona Gale's political interests.

FOLLETT, WILSON. *Zona Gale: An Artist in Fiction* (New York, 1923). A pamphlet assessing her work through *Miss Lulu Bett*.

GARD, ROBERT. *Grassroots Theater: A Search for Regional Arts in America* (Madison, 1955). Enlightening discussion of Zona Gale's activity in small-town theater productions.

GARLAND, HAMLIN. *My Friendly Contemporaries* (New York, 1932) and *Afternoon Neighbors* (New York, 1934). Brief but charming reminiscences about Zona Gale.

HERRON, IMA HONAKER. *The Small Town in American Literature* (New York, 1959). Excellent analysis of Zona Gale's fiction and its place in American literature.

HOFFMAN, FREDERICK J. *The Twenties: American Writing in the Postwar Decade* (New York, 1955). Provocative treatment of Zona Gale's position in Middle West realism.

HOLLOWAY, JEAN. *Hamlin Garland* (Austin, Texas, 1960). Describes Garland's role in the selection of *Miss Lulu Bett* (the play) for the Pulitzer Prize.

KRUTCH, JOSEPH WOOD. "Zona Gale's New Manner," *Nation*, CXXIX (Dec. 11, 1929), 725. Review of *Borgia* and notations about her later development.

KUNITZ, STANLEY J., AND HAYCRAFT, HOWARD, eds. *Twentieth Century Authors: A Biographical Dictionary of American Authors* (New York, 1942).

LA FOLLETTE, BELLE CASE AND FOLA. *Robert M. La Follette*, 2 vols. (New York, 1935). Definitive biography of Wisconsin's Robert La Follette, Sr. Includes important references to Zona Gale's association with the La Follette family.

LAKE, I. C. "Zona Gale's Home Becomes Library," *Library Journal*, LXX (Dec. 15, 1945), 1201-2. An account of the Breese home on MacFarlane Road reconverted into the Portage Public Library.

LEWISOHN, LUDWIG. "Native Plays," *Nation*, CXII (Feb. 2, 1921), 189. Provocative review of *Miss Lulu Bett* (the play) and its contribution to American drama.

LOIZEAUX, M. D. "Talking Shop," *Wilson Library Bulletin,* XXI (November, 1946), 243. Brief discussion of Zona Gale's association with Wisconsin State Senator George Standenmeyer and legislative librarian Charles McCarthy.

MICHAUD, RÉGIS. *The American Novel To-Day* (Boston, 1928). Routine summary of the Friendship Village and Lulu Bett periods.

OVERTON, GRANT. *American Nights Entertainment* (New York, 1923) and *The Women Who Make Our Novels* (New York, 1931). Biographical sketches and perfunctory criticism.

QUINN, ARTHUR H. *American Fiction: An Historical and Critical Survey* (New York, 1936). Necessarily brief but sharply incisive summary of Zona Gale's fiction.

ROURKE, CONSTANCE. "Transitions," *New Republic,* XXIII (Aug. 11, 1920), 315-16. Review of *Peace in Friendship Village* and indispensable analysis of Zona Gale's whole Friendship Village cycle.

SALZMAN, MAURICE. *Plagiarism: The "Art" of Stealing Literary Material* (Los Angeles, 1931). Informative account of Zona Gale's experience with a plagiarist.

SIMONSON, HAROLD P. "Zona Gale's Acquaintance with Francis Grierson," *The Historical Society of Southern California Quarterly,* XLI (March, 1959), 11-16. Explanation of Francis Grierson's occultistic influence upon Miss Gale, who visited him in California shortly before he died in 1927.

SUMNER, KEENE. "The Everlasting Persistence of This Western Girl," *The American Magazine,* XCI (June, 1921), 34-35, 137-41. A warmly sympathetic portrayal of Zona Gale.

TOWNE, CHARLES HANSON. *Adventures in Editing* (New York, 1926). An autobiography including a full account of Zona Gale's winning *The Delineator* short-story prize in 1910.

UNTERMEYER, LOUIS. *Heavens* (New York, 1922). An anecdotal autobiography with an amusing parody on Zona Gale's double ending for *Miss Lulu Bett* (the play).

VAN DOREN, CARL. *Contemporary American Novelists* (New York, 1928) and *The American Novel 1789-1939* (New York, 1940). Both books discuss Zona Gale as a Middle West realist.

Index

Abbott, Grace, 61, 126
Adamic, Louis, 55
Adams, Brooks, 91
Adams, Charles Kendall, 68
Adams, Henry, 34, 95, 109
Adams, Samuel Hopkins, 70
Addams, Jane, 24, 34, 50, 57, 58, 61, 68, 71, 126, 137
Ade, George, 70
Aegis, The (University of Wisconsin), 23
Alcott, Louisa May, 22
Alexander, Grand Duke of Russia, 94, 134
Anderson, Sherwood, 15, 16, 18, 24, 80, 103
Andreyev, Leonid, 113
Anthony, Susan B., 64
Arnold, Edwin, 94
Arnold, Matthew, 91
Astor, John Jacob, 21
Atherton, Gertrude, 28, 70
Atlantic Monthly, 47, 121
Austen, Jane, 40
Austin, Mary, 50, 59, 70

Bacon, Francis, 17
Bailey, Alice, 102
Bascom, John, 68, 69
Baudelaire, Charles, 33
Beach, Rex, 70
Beard, Mary R., 126
Beardsley, Aubrey, 33
Beck, L. Adams, 97
Bellamy, Edward, 67, 94
Benchley, Robert, 79, 83
Bergson, Henri, 116
Berkeley, George, 94
Besant, Annie, 96
Beveridge, Albert, 68

Bigelow, William Sturgis, 95
Birge, E. A., 128
Blackmore, R. D., 22
Blaine, John, 22, 128
Blavatsky, Madame H. P., 94, 96, 99, 117
Bloser, Parker, 107
Blyton, W. J., 103
Bowen, Louise DeKoven, 61
Bragdon, Claude, 95, 105
Brandeis, Louis, 71
Breckenridge, Sophonsiba P., 61, 62
Breese, Juliette (daughter of William L.), 17, 125
Breese, Leslyn (adopted daughter of William L. and Zone Gale Breese), 17, 125
Breese, William L. (husband of Zona Gale), 17, 125, 127
Breese, Mrs. William L. (*see* Zona Gale), 125ff.
Brooks, Van Wyck, 91
Broun, Heywood, 85, 86, 91
Browne, Porter Emerson, 70, 86
Brownson, Orestes, 94
Bryan, William Jennings, 57, 67, 68
Buck, J. D., 97
Buck, Pearl, 133
Bulwer-Lytton, Edward, 22
Bunyan, John, 22
Burgess, Frank Gelett, 28
Burnett, Francis, 22
Burns, Lucy, 64
Burroughs, John, 25

Calverton, V. F., 91
Camus, Albert, 88
Cardinal (University of Wisconsin), 23, 54
Carlyle, Thomas, 115

Carnegie, Andrew, 57
Cather, Willa, 15, 16, 24, 27, 79, 91, 101, 103
Catt, Carrie Chapman, 57
Century Magazine, 83, 91, 106
Chamberlain, Neville, 59, 137
Chamberlain, Thomas, 68
Chew, Samuel, 103
Christian Century, 133
Cobb, Irvin S., 70
Collier's, 106
Commons, John R., 53, 68
Comstock, Anthony, 93
Comte, Auguste, 94
Coolidge, Calvin, 55, 71, 72
Cooper, James Fenimore, 109, 110, 111
Cornell Dramatic Club, 43
Costigan, Mabel, 71
Courtney, Robert, 97, 117-18
Crane, Stephen, 27, 111
Craven, Frank, 86
Cummins, Albert, 68

Damrosch, Walter, 25
Darrow, Clarence, 68
Darwin, Charles, 17, 94
Davidson, Donald, 120, 121
Davis, Jefferson, 21
Davis, John W., 72
de Forest, Marian, 126
Delineator, The, 42, 83, 87; prize, 42-43
Dell, Floyd, 24, 55, 60
Democrat (Portage), 23
Derleth, August, 22, 26
Dewey, John, 68
Dickens, Charles, 22
Dickinson, Emily, 25
Dickinson, Thomas, 43
Donnelly, Ignatius, 67
Dos Passos, John, 24, 55
Dreiser, Theodore, 33, 75, 98, 104, 111
Drier, Mary, 71
Drummond, A. M., 43
Drummond, William, 17

Dunbar, Olivia Howard, 31
Duncan, Isadora, 25

Eckhart, Meister, 97
Eddy, Mary Baker, 95, 96
Edison, Thomas A., 98
Eggleston, Edward, 15
Eighteenth Amendment, 54
Einstein, Albert, 95
Eliot, George, 22
Eliot, T. S., 45, 139
Ellis, Edith, 99
Ely, Richard T., 68
Emerson, Ralph Waldo, 17, 78, 94, 116, 138
Evening Wisconsin (Milwaukee), 24
Evening World (New York), 24, 25, 26
Everybody's, 42, 47, 49

Faulkner, William, 57, 105, 106, 111, 112, 114
Ferber, Edna, 24
Fisher, Dorothy Canfield, 50
Fitzgerald, Edward, 27
Fitzgerald, F. Scott, 89
Flaubert, Gustave, 33
Follett, Wilson, 79
Forster, E. M., 115
Forum, 72
Frank, Glenn, 55, 83, 128-31, 132, 135
Frankfurter, Felix, 71
Frazer, James, 94
Freud, Sigmund, 94
Fuller, Margaret, 59, 94

Gale, Charles (father of Zona Gale), 16, 17, 18, 20, 22, 36
Gale, Eliza (mother of Zona Gale), 16, 17, 18-20, 25, 28-31, 36, 43, 47, 99-100
Gale, Zona, writings of:
"Allotropes," 116-17
"Autobiography," 106

Index

"Beauty and the Commonplace, The," 115-16
"Bella," 106
"Biggest Business, The," 46
"Bill," 106
"Biography of Blade," 106
Birth, 47, 49, 63, 73-78, 88, 104, 105 107, 120, 135
Borgia, 56, 119-21, 135
"Brendy," 122
Bridal Pond, 121-23, 135
"Bridal Pond," 122-23
"Cable, The," 48
"Charivari, The," 106
"Cherries," 106
Christmas, 37, 50
"Civic Improvemnt in the Little Towns," 43-44
Clouds, The (play), 126
"Cobweb, The," 121
"Conservatives' Paradise," 72
"Conversation," 112
"Correspondence Drafting La Follette," 72
"Crime of the Ages, The," 58
Daughter of the Morning, A, 46-47, 62-63, 80
"Dime, The," 122
"Dream," 47
"Earth Mother," 45
"Ernie Mendenhall," 106-7
Evening Clothes (play), 126, 127
"Exit Charity," 46
Faint Perfume, 16, 38, 63, 83, 87, 88-91, 104, 111, 122, 135
Faint Perfume (play), 128
"Feast of Nations, The," 48
Flight of Clouds, 19
Frank Miller of Mission Inn, 133-34
Friendship Village, 37, 45
Friendship Village Love Stories, 37
"Great Black House, The," 45
Heart's Kindred, 46, 57-58
"Here! Here! Here!," 121
"Implications," 112
"Jailbird," 121

"La Follette's Vindication," 72
"Last Night," 106
Light Woman, 131-32, 134
Loves of Pelleas and Etarre, The, 35-36
Magna, 134-35
Man at Red Barns, 83, 86, 87
Miss Lulu Bett, 16, 38, 49, 63, 78-84, 86, 87, 88, 103, 104, 111, 135, 136
Miss Lulu Bett (play), 84-87, 107
Mister Pitt (play), 107
Mothers to Men, 37, 50
Neighborhood Stories, 37, 38, 39, 41, 42, 45, 46
Neighbors, The (play), 37, 43, 50, 84, 107
"Novel and the Spirit, The," 112-15
"Novel of Tomorrow, The," 112-15
Old Fashioned Tales, 128
"Outlaw War Now!," 58
Papa La Fleur, 127-28, 131, 134
Peace in Friendship Village, 37, 40-41, 46, 47-50
Portage, Wisconsin and Other Essays, 109-19, 125
Preface to a Life, 19, 63, 78, 91, 93, 99, 101-6, 111, 121, 135
"Reception Surprise, The," 47
Romance Island, 34-35, 36
"Scholarship and the Spirit," 115, 116-17, 119
The Secret Way (poetry), 87-88, 107
"Springtime," 121
"Story of Jeffro, The," 47, 49-50
"Tattie," 121
"Tea Party, The," 45
"Time Has Come, The," 45
"Tobacco Shop," 122
"Two Summaries," 117, 118
Uncle Jimmy (play), 87, 107
"United States and the Artist," 109-12
"What Women Won in Wisconsin," 64-65

When I Was a Little Girl, 37, 45
"When the Hero Came Home," 48
"White Bread," 121
"Why I Shall Vote for La Follette," 72
"Wisconsin Note-Book," 122
Yellow Gentians and Blue, 106, 107, 121
Galton, Francis, 94
Gandhi, Mahatma, 93
Garland, Hamlin, 15, 24, 47, 53, 70, 86, 98, 99, 111
Gaskell, Elizabeth, 40
Gautier, Theophile, 27
George, Henry, 67
Ginn, Edward, 57
Gladden, Washngton, 68
Glasgow, Ellen, 27
Glaspell, Susan, 50
Gold, Michael, 55
Grey, Zane, 73
Grierson, Francis, 98, 99, 105
Gurdjieff, George Ivanovich, 94, 105

Hagedorn, Herman, 70
Haggard, Rider, 22
Hall, Gilman, 47, 49
Hamilton, Dr. Alice, 61
Hapgood, Norman, 71
Hardy, Thomas, 76
Harper's Monthly, 42, 134
Hawthorne, Nathaniel, 22, 94, 109, 110, 111, 138
Heard, Gerald, 95
Hearn, Lafcadio, 95
Hemingway, Ernest, 112, 114, 138
Heywood, Rosalind, 98
Hitler, Adolf, 137
Hoffman, Frederick J., 96, 103
Holmes, John Haynes, 58, 96
Holmes, Oliver Wendell, 94
Howard, Sidney, 55
Howe, S. W., 15, 38, 74
Howells, William Dean, 24, 27, 33, 36, 91, 94, 98, 111, 114
Hull House, 24, 60-61, 62
Huneker, James, 33

Huntington, Henry, 133
Hurst, Fannie, 40, 55, 82
Huxley, Thomas, 94
Hyman, Ralph B., 135

International Congress of Women, 126
Irving, Washington, 109, 136
Irwin, Will, 28

James, Henry, 30, 36, 82, 94, 99, 105, 109, 110, 111, 114, 115
James, William, 50
Jewett, Rutger, 79
Jewett, Sarah Orne, 27
Johnson, Mary, 113, 114
Joliet, Jean, 20
Jordan, David Starr, 55
Josephson, Matthew, 91
Journal (Milwaukee), 24, 126
Joyce, James, 105, 112
Jung, Carl, 95

Kafka, Franz, 105
Kant, Immanuel, 94
Kelley, Florence, 61, 71
Kellogg, Frank, 70
Kenny, Mary E., 61
Keyes, E. W., 66
Khayyam, Omar, 27
Kidd, Benjamin, 97
Kingsley, Charles, 22
Kirkland, Joseph, 15
Krishnamurti, 94, 105
Kronenberger, Louis, 103
Krutch, Joseph Wood, 55, 119

Ladies' Home Journal, 87
La Farge, John, 95
La Follette, Philip, 126, 127-31
La Follette, Robert M., 52, 54, 57, 61, 66-72
La Follette, Jr., Robert M., 51, 71, 130
La Follette's Magazine, 51, 57, 66, 67

Lathrop, Julia C., 61
Latimer, Margery, 56
Lawrence, D. H., 28, 89, 102, 112
Le Gallienne, Richard, 25-26, 30-31, 33
Lewis, Sinclair, 16, 38, 74, 79, 86, 101, 103, 110, 111, 137
Lewisohn, Ludwig, 84, 85
Lincoln, Abraham, 39, 99; Mrs. Lincoln and "Tad," 21
Liveright, Horace, 55
Lloyd, Beatrice Demarest and David, 26, 68
Lodge, Henry Cabot, 70, 72
Lodge, Sir Oliver, 95
Loti, Pierre, 33
Lovett, Robert Morss, 55, 86
Lowell, Amy, 27
Lowell, Percival, 95
Lubbock, Percy, 115

Maeterlinck, Maurice, 27, 28
Mallarmé, Stephané, 33, 116
Mansfield, Katherine, 105
Marinetti, Filippo Tommaso, 102
Marquette, Father, 20
Masters, Edgar Lee, 15, 87
McAllister, Ward, 28
McCarthy, Charles, 51
McDowell, Mary E., 61, 62
McKinley, William, 68
Meikeljohn, Alexander, 129
Melville, Herman, 27, 110, 111, 138
Mencken, H. L., 38, 86, 90, 103, 129, 130
Meyer, Ernest L., 129
Michaud, Régis, 75
Millay, Edna St. Vincent, 55
Miller, Frank, 96, 105, 125, 131, 133-34
Monroe, Harriet, 26
Moody, William Vaughn, 26
Mount Mary College, 126
Muir, John, 21

Naguchi, Yone, 26, 131, 134
Nation, 64, 71, 72

New Republic, 72
New Thought movement, 87, 96-99
Nineteenth Amendment, 59, 64
Norris, Frank, 34
Norris, George, 68
Norris, Kathleen, 73, 111

O'Brien, Edward J., 106
O'Neill, Eugene, 85
Orage, A. R., 105
O'Reilly, Leonora, 61
Oskison, John, 42
Ouspensky, P. D., 93, 95, 105, 117
Outing, 26
Outlook, The, 42

Pacifism, 56-59
Parker, Dorothy, 55
Parrington, Vernon Lewis, 68
Pater, Walter, 116
Paul, Alice, 64
Pavlov, Ivan, 94
Payne, Henry, 66
Pemberton, Brock, 84
Perkins, Frances, 126
Pfister, Charles, 66
Plato, 17
Poe, Edgar Allan, 110
Porter, Katherine Anne, 55
Progressivism, 51-52, 54, 56, 58, 66-72, 131, 136
Proust, Marcel, 105, 112
Pulitzer Prize, won by Zona Gale, 16, 71, 84, 85-86

Quinn, Arthur, 74

Rauschenbush, Walter, 53, 68
Rawleigh, W. T., 71
Rice, Elmer, 55
Riis, Jacob, 41
Ripon College, 58, 126
Robinson, Edward Arlington, 26, 74
Robinson, Joseph, 70
Roe, E. P., 22
Rogers, Edith, 22

Rollins College, 126
Rölvaag, Ole, 16
Roosevelt, Franklin D., 59; Mrs. Roosevelt, 126
Roosevelt, Theodore, 69, 70, 72
Rossetti, Dante Gabriel, 27, 28
Rourke, Constance, 40, 41, 47, 79-80
Runge, Clara T., 130
Russell, Dora, 129, 130

Sacco and Vanzetti movement, 54-55
Salsman, Maurice, 107
Saltus, Edgar, 33
Sandburg, Carl, 62
Santayana, George, 100
Sartre, Jean-Paul, 88, 113
Saurat, Denis, 117, 118
Sawyer, Philetus, 66, 67
Schorer, Mark, 56
Scott, Sir Walter, 22
Scribner's, 119, 121
Scudder, Vida, 55
Sedgwick, Anne Douglas, 50, 113, 114
Sedgwick, Ellery, 47
Shakespeare, William, 17
Shaw, George Bernard, 91
Sherman, Stuart, 86
Sinclair, May, 113
Sinclair, Upton, 34, 55, 98, 104
Skinner, B. F., 44
Smart Set, 26
Smith, J. Allen, 68
Smith, Mary Robert, 61
Spencer, Herbert, 17, 94
Spiritualism, 99-101
Spooner, John, 66
Standenmeyer, George, 51
Stanton, Elizabeth Cady, 64
Starr, Ellen Gates, 61, 62
Stedman, Clarence Edmund, 26, 27, 29, 30, 33, 34, 35
Steffens, Lincoln, 42
Steinbeck, John, 36, 104
Stratton-Porter, Gene, 73, 111
Street, Julian, 70

Success, 26
Suckow, Ruth, 16, 24, 38
Suffrage movement, 64-65
Sumner, Keene, 20, 84
Swedenborg, Emanuel, 17
Swinburne, Charles, 27, 91

Taft, William Howard, 69
Tagore, Rabindranath, 94, 97, 134
Taine, Hippolyte, 94
Tarbell, Ida M., 55
Tarkington, Booth, 70
Taylor, Zachery, 21
Teasdale, Sara, 27
Thackery, William, 22
Thomas, Norman, 105
Thoreau, Henry David, 90
Torrence, Ridgely, 18, 26-31, 33, 99, 126, 135
Towne, Charles Hanson, 26, 42-43, 70
Turner, Frederick Jackson, 21
Twain, Mark, 91, 114, 117

Underhill, Evelyn, 97
Unity, 58, 97
Untermeyer, Louis, 25, 85

Van Doren, Carl, 16, 55, 56, 79, 91
Van Gogh, Vincent, 102
Van Hise, Charles R., 68, 70
Van Vechten, Carl, 16
Veblen, Thorstein, 50, 68, 93
Villard, Oswald Garrison, 71
Vivas, Eliseo, 56
Volstead Act, 54

Wagner, Richard, 116
Wallace, Lew, 22
Walton, E. H., 131
Ward, Lester, 93
Watson, J. B., 117
Weeks, John, 70
Wells, H. G., 91

Wescott, Glenway, 24, 38, 56
Wharton, Edith, 36, 50, 79, 82-83,
    86, 91, 110, 114
Wheeler, Burton K., 72
White, William Allen, 74
Whitehead, Alfred North, 95
Whitman, Walt, 39, 78, 97, 99, 102,
    118, 136
Wiggin, Kate Douglas, 73
Wilde, Oscar, 25, 28, 33, 34, 91
Willard, Frances, 53, 54
Wilson, Woodrow, 57
Wisconsin Dramatic Society, 43, 84
Wisconsin, University of, 22-23, 43,
    61, 68-70, 126, 128-31
Wollstonecraft, Mary, 59
Woman's Home Companion, The,
    42
Woolcott, Alexander, 85
Woolf, Virginia, 112, 115
Women's rights, 59-66
World Tomorrow, 72

Yale Review, 116
Youth's Companion, 22

Zola, Emile, 33

Date Due

	PRINTED	IN U. S. A.	